The Joy Bringer Challenge

THE **JOY**
BRINGER
Challenge

LIVING THE POWER
OF THE GOOD NEWS

Season Bowers

NASHVILLE

NEW YORK • LONDON • MELBOURNE • VANCOUVER

THE **JOY** BRINGER Challenge

LIVING THE POWER OF THE GOOD NEWS

Published in New York, New York, by Morgan James Publishing. Morgan James is a trademark of Morgan James, LLC. www.MorganJamesPublishing.com

Proudly distributed by Ingram Publisher Services.

A **FREE** ebook edition is available for you
or a friend with the purchase of this print book.

_____

CLEARLY SIGN YOUR NAME ABOVE

Instructions to claim your free ebook edition:
1. Visit MorganJamesBOGO.com
2. Sign your name CLEARLY in the space above
3. Complete the form and submit a photo of this entire page
4. You or your friend can download the ebook to your preferred device

ISBN 9781636980782 paperback
ISBN 9781636980799 ebook
Library of Congress Control Number:
2022948077

Cover Design by:
Rachel Lopez
www.r2cdesign.com

Interior Design by:
Chris Treccani
www.3dogcreative.net

Morgan James is a proud partner of Habitat for Humanity Peninsula
and Greater Williamsburg. Partners in building since 2006.

Get involved today! Visit: www.morgan-james-publishing.com/giving-back

My eternal Joy Bringer, Jesus.
Because of your goodness and for your glory.

Acknowledgments

This book would not exist without Jesus. my true and constant joy. Through him, others contributed in powerful ways which hold my eternal gratitude.

Rachel Hanson, thank you for listening to the nudge of the Lord and generously sending me to my first writers conference where it all began.

Lynn Donovan, thank you for speaking life and believing in me. Marcy Rossi, your dreams and gifts helped make an idea come to life.

Doc and Beth Maranville, you put air under my voice to carry it out to the world. I'm humbled by your love and support.

Gina Holm, thank you for your kindness and simple prayer. Laying hands on me and releasing your testimony changed everything. Look what God did!

To Terry Whalin, you sought me out and filled me with so much joy! Thank you for believing in me and not listening to all the reasons I gave you to not publish my book.

I am so grateful for my dear friends who challenged me to push beyond the fear and let the Lord move in ways I never imagined. To the ones who gave, thank you.

To the anonymous one who secretly paid the bill that felt like a mountain, I wish I knew who you are so I could look you in the eye and thank you. My hug would be awkwardly long, and my tears would get on your shoulder, but you could see and feel the depth of my gratitude. May you be doubly blessed in return.

Courtney, you are the absolute shizzle.

To those who joined me to lend their passion and expertise to the first 15 Day Joy Bringer Challenge on Facebook, (Michael Koulianos, Stuart Macklin, Andrew Hopkins, Sadie and Chad Roberts, Tracy Brown, Aeron Brown, Heather Sanford, Ann Hansen, Glenn Prior, and Kris Bowers), thank you. Your wisdom, passion, and investment laid the foundation for this book.

To my agent, Stephanie Alton. You are a treasure! You believed in me from the beginning. You guided me down a long road with tender courage and deep conviction. Thank you for not giving up on me.

Being on the radio is a bizarre thing. As an actor on the stage, you have the benefit of an immediate audience reaction, but there is no way to know if what you say on the radio really has an effect. As much as it is frustrating to not gage the response, I also love that I will never know how the Lord chooses to use my daily offering. It's none of my business and I trust that God will do infinitely more than I can imagine. To the radio stations who generously give me the chance to speak to your listeners, thank you. It's an honor to be a part of your ministry.

Morgan James Publishing, your yes turned my mourning into dancing. Every single person I have had the pleasure of working with has filled me with so much joy! I am humbled and grateful.

My beloved husband, Kris with a K. "But isn't that how the story goes?" Every step of the way you have held me with your love (and side control). Through the pain, struggle, accomplishment, and celebration, you are the one I want in my guard. Adventure is best with you and there is so much more ahead. I choose you, babe.

TABLE OF CONTENTS

Chapter 1:

Meet Joy

Joy Verse

"Be cheerful with joyous celebration in every season of life.
Let your joy overflow!"–Philippians 4:4 TPT

Joy is for you.

It's true. Despite what you may believe, what you have heard, or may be hearing right now inside your head, the truth remains that abundant, consistent, and lasting joy is for you. I'm guessing there is something in you that wants this to be true. You want more. Or maybe you want to be able to live out the joy that you experience in a productive way. I have been there. But it's also possible that you need some more reasons to believe this bold statement. You need something to hold on to and guide you as you maneuver through the obstacle course of life. I have also been there.

My name is Season. It's not Summer, Susan, or Seasons. It's Season. I hated my name when I was little. Having an uncommon name is pretty much an open invitation for teasing from kids, and adults aren't much better. Experiencing the teacher call roll on the first day of school was the worst. Reading my name aloud was a cue for snickers and a variation of, "What kind of a name is that?" My parents never gave me a good reason as to why they chose such a strange name. They simply said, "We just liked it." That doesn't suffice when mean kids, or insensitive adults retort with a cutting and never clever response. It wasn't until I was older that my mother told me they named me Season because of Ecclesiastes 3:1, "To everything there is a season and a time for every purpose under heaven." She explained that I came at just the right time in their lives. I finally had a "why" to help me understand, and since then I've been inspired by the significance of the Lord's timing and how He really does have a good plan for our lives.

Understanding the "why" of things gives us a handle to hold. When I knew a bit more about why I had such a bizarre name, I gained confidence. I could respond to the questions and the negative comments with my head held high knowing that there was indeed a reason with a powerful truth behind it. There really is a season and a time for every purpose under heaven, and in some small way, I am a walking, talking representation of that truth.

Speaking of seasons, this is your season to grow in joy. My desire is that our journey together here will be a catalyst in your life. That you will discover more about who the Lord is, what he's done for you, and what that means for your life. I want you to get all that Jesus Christ paid for and live like the gospel is good news. Because it is! And that good news brings great and powerful joy.

Jesus was the most joyful person ever to live and he has invited you to receive his joy and go out into the world. But just like the people who would snap back at hearing my name with a comment like, "Were your parents on drugs?" or "What kind of a name is that?" I understand that without a clear understanding of what joy is and how you get it, there is doubt and judgement. People didn't understand my name without the why, and it's very possible that you find it difficult to believe that joy is for you without the "what" or "why" either.

Meet Joy

C.S. Lewis said, "Joy is the serious business of heaven." Joy is mentioned in some form 472 times in the Bible and yet it is often overlooked and misunderstood. Joy isn't happiness, but it's closely related. Joy also isn't only an emotion, although it can be very emotional. It's not automatic. Instead, joy is a choice. It's also a result of the presence of God.

Joy is not an option in the Christian life. As Levi Lusko said in an Instagram post, "Joy is the flag that flies high when the King of our hearts is in residence there." In my search I have found that most definitions fall short of my understanding and personal experience regarding joy. I want to begin by presenting to you my effort in defining joy: "A buoyant sense of well-being because of the person and work of Jesus Christ, cultivated by the power and presence of the Holy Spirit, and because of the love of the Father."

Because of the steadfast love and faithfulness of God we can always have joy. Philippians 4:4 (TPT) says, "Be cheerful with joyous celebration in every season of life. Let your joy overflow!" In *every* season? Even through the pain, tragedy, hardship, strife, and doubt? Yes. But in order to do that we've got to really understand the "why's" and "how's" of joy.

There are four major areas that I believe are vital for us to understand so we can live full of joy and be Joy Bringers wherever we go: 1) the gift of salvation, 2) the healing available to us, 3) the filling of the Holy Spirit, and 4) the leading our lives and leading of others around us, from a place of purpose and joy. This book is divided into these four sections. Each section will reveal truth that will shatter the misconceptions about joy and Jesus. It will also help you to leave behind things like doubt, bitterness, pain, shame, and limitations to help you live with lasting joy.

At the end of each section is a chapter that will give you a corresponding core value relating to that section. Joy Bringer's Core Values are joy handles, if you will, to help you hold on to and maintain your joy when things get tough in everyday life. Throughout this experience, you will be challenged to practice the tools and principles of being a Joy Bringer.

Becoming a Joy Bringer means being filled with the joy of the Lord and thinking, looking, and acting more like Jesus, who was the original Joy Bringer.

I'm so excited for your journey to joy! I believe that the Lord has led you to this moment, and he has wholeness and freedom for you as you receive His joy and bring it into the world. Let's go!

A JOY FILLED BLESSING

I bless you, in Jesus's name, to begin this journey with confidence in your good and loving Father in Heaven. I bless you to know that this process is covered in the kindness and love of the Holy Spirit, so fear is not welcome to stay. I bless you to say "yes" to the invitation of Jesus to follow him and be a Joy Bringer to your home, your work, your city, and the world.

Section 1:

The Joy of Our Salvation

Joy verse:
"Restore to me the joy of Your salvation, and uphold me
by Your generous Spirit."–Psalm 51:12 NKJV

Joy Principle:
Joy is for you because Jesus is for you.

Joy Bringer's Core Value:
Gratitude is the gateway to joy.

Joy begins with Jesus—He is the source. In order to receive the gift
of joy that I know Jesus has for you, it's vital that you understand
the package it comes in— salvation.

This section will take you on a journey to understand who
Jesus is and what he accomplished on your behalf. That's where
the good news comes in, good news that brings great joy. The formal word is *salvation*. It's a big word used to describe something
even bigger. Most people think of salvation as the forgiveness of
sin because of Jesus's death on the cross and its power to save us

from eternal separation from God in hell. But that's only a fraction of what comes with salvation!

The word *gospel* means good news. The depth and breadth of salvation is brought to us through Jesus's birth, life, death, and resurrection. It's not just good news for the future, but for right here and now. But before we begin to really grab hold of it, I want to ask you a simple question: Have you been saved?

We often use the word "saved," or "born again" to describe our new reality when we say "yes" to Jesus and give him our lives. That "yes" changes everything. It frees us from the weight and punishment of sin. It identifies us as a son or daughter of the King, our Father in Heaven who created us and who delights over us. It leads us into a new life that is marked by freedom and joy. It gives us the authority and power to live a life of victory. And it guarantees an eternal life in the presence of God in Heaven. That's a lot of goodness! So why isn't every Christian living full of joy?

The problem that I've seen is that many who say yes to Jesus don't collect on the full offer of salvation. They are drawn in by the promise of eternal life and forgiveness of sin, but they don't take advantage of the fullness of the gift. New life. Power to live. Joy overflowing. The gospel is meant to change our lives and the lives of those around us. That is what it means to be a Joy Bringer—one who lives like the gospel is good news.

So, I ask again, have you been saved? If so, I can't wait to help you grab hold of the joy that is for you because of the gift you have received. If not, read on...there is a gift just for you. That's good news!

Chapter 2:

Joy is for You

Joy verse

"Those who listen to instruction will prosper; those who trust the Lord will be joyful."–Proverbs 16:20 NLT

The greatest love story ever told. No, it's not the latest tearjerker to hit the big screen, it's the story of you and God. You may not be aware of it, but it began a long time ago, and much of the backstory is recorded in the Bible. There were many twists and turns to get to you and in order to really understand the scope and impact of your love story you've got to know how it came about.

It began with love. Before the creation of the universe the Father, Son, and Holy Spirit had a good thing going. They knew love, they were love, and they wanted to share it. The Bible tells the story of God and his people, and just like any good story it's full of drama. The many twists and turns in the story are all brought about by choices. The choice to eat the forbidden fruit, the choice to worship other gods, the choice to stand up for what is right, and the choice to trust the voice of God. From the beginning, humans were given freewill and the ability to make choices.

They made the choice to sin, to defy God, and to turn away. That choice had great consequence and placed a barrier between a Holy God and his creation, that's the problem of sin.

When sin first entered the picture, there became a separation between humans and God. Adam and Eve did the one thing the Lord asked them not to, and immediately in fear and shame they hid from him. Because their actions carried consequences, their perfect existence with the Father in the Garden of Eden came to an end. But that punishment didn't come with rage and anger. In fact, the consequence came with a plan—a loving promise to rescue and restore their relationship, and it was going to come through the birth of a baby.

The Hero

Any good drama requires a hero, someone to save the day. The hero in this story is Jesus. While he wasn't fully revealed until Act 2 (the New Testament), his presence and the promise of his birth can be seen from the very first page and foretold throughout Act 1 (the Old Testament). He was the baby referred to in the first promise and his accomplishments were the ones foretold (Genesis 3:15). His reputation preceded him, but no one expected him. No one thought to look for him in Bethlehem. No one thought he'd be born to an unmarried virgin. No one knew to look to a baby born in a stable to save the world.

A friend of mine was pregnant with her first child and, like most parents-to-be, she and her husband were consumed by the worries of "How are we going to do this?" They couldn't see how they would possibly have enough money, time, energy, and love to pull off the role of being parents. My friend's grandmother told her, "Honey, don't you know that every baby comes with a loaf of bread under their arm?" This is an old Hebrew saying (and often found in Spanish speaking cultures) meaning that parents need not worry about the costs to feed and raise a child because God will provide a way. It's true! The Lord is so good at providing a way when we can't see one.

Baby Jesus was born with a loaf of bread for the entire world! In fact, he was born in Bethlehem, which, when translated, means "the house of bread." Jesus says of himself in John 6:35, "I am the bread of life; whoever comes to me shall not hunger, and whoever believes in me shall never thirst." He compared his own body to bread as he broke a loaf and said, "This is my body given for you..." (Matthew 26:26). He was the bread that not only would satisfy the world, but he said of himself, "I am the way, the truth, and the life. No one comes to the Father except through me" (John 14:6). Jesus came to make a way. He is the way. He came for you.

The bread that Jesus brought to us was salvation, the fulfillment of the long- awaited promise. But before we get to the part of salvation that we typically think of, the forgiveness of our sins through his death on the cross, there is an important part of salvation found in his birth.

Promise keeper

Are you a promise keeper? Does it make you crazy when people don't keep their promises? Unfulfilled promises can cause great disappointment, even anger and pain. As children, the promises of our parents hold a lot of weight. I didn't have any children of my own when I married my husband. We met and married ten weeks later, and I became an insta-mom to his three daughters who were 6, 8, and 10. Talk about a crash course in parenting! Being a mom made me quickly aware of the words that came out of my mouth. The casual statements, "Sure, we can go get frozen yogurt after school" or "Yes, we can go see the puppies at the store tomorrow," weren't quickly forgotten! "*You promised!*" would ring out from the backseat. Yes, I did, and I wanted to be true to my word. I wanted them to trust me.

Our Father in heaven always had a plan to fulfill his promise to his children through the gift of his son. In fact, the Father, Son, and Holy Spirit were all in on it. That promise sustained the Israelites for hundreds of years. It saw them through hundreds of years, through the wilderness, wars, famine, captivity, and silence. While the Israelites waited for centuries, the Lord was faithful and loving to reveal that plan in many ways, through many people, and at the right time, it was fulfilled through the birth of a baby. The birth of Jesus was the fulfilment of a long-awaited promise of God to His people.

Jesus didn't only bring freedom and joy to the Israelites. Isaiah 49:5-6 indicates that while Jesus was in the womb the plan was for him to also be a light to the Gentiles and all people to the ends of the earth. He fulfilled a promise to you too—a promise you may not even know you were waiting for. His birth brought joy to you by answering your cry to be saved. The Lord heard you. When you lost hope, he answered. When you cried out in fear, he answered. When you were abandoned and alone, he answered. He answered you by being born.

The Father's one and only son entered this world to save *you*. While you may not have felt it in that moment, your cry for help was heard and answered. Even though that answer came over 2,000 years ago, it is supernaturally effective in this very moment—as if in your exact moment of need the baby Jesus was born just for you. If the angel who, at the birth of Jesus proclaimed, "Do not be afraid; for behold, I bring you good news of great joy" (Luke 2:10) was saying it to *you*.

What a love story! God has loved you from the very beginning. There is nothing you can do to change his love for you. The Lord longs for you to know the depth and breadth of his love. His faithfulness extends to every area of your life. This is really good news. News intended to fill you with so much joy that you feel you can take on the world.

The Antagonist

The enemy is afraid. He knows that God is faithful, and he can't change that, so instead he wants to convince you that you are somehow the exception. The enemy wants you to believe you aren't good enough or have been disqualified from the fullness of God's love and promise. He uses the painful wounds of disappointment and rejection caused by the unfulfilled promises of those we have loved and trusted. If the enemy can get us to project our fears onto the Father in heaven to keep us from receiving the fullness of God's promise, then the enemy gets the point (not the win).

The good news is, God is victorious. He is on a mission to reveal more of himself to you so you can grow in your trust and confidence. God is holy. He isn't able to be anything other than good. God is love. He is trustworthy. He created you. God knows your every thought, feeling, desire, and fear. He wants to draw you close and fill you with that blessed assurance that all of his goodness is for you.

Proverbs 16:20 says, "Those who listen to instruction will prosper, *those who trust the Lord **will be joyful**"* (emphasis added). Joy is a promise, a gift that comes with your trust. He is worthy to be trusted with every area of your life. This is what makes all the difference. Many Christians stop at only trusting God with their eternity. While that's great, it's not the full offer.

The Greek word *sozo* is where we get the word "saved" or "salvation." It means rescue, deliverance, and wholeness. The salvation of the Lord includes rescue from the death sentence and bondage of sin, made whole—a new creation in Christ Jesus, filled full of joy, and empowered to share that joy with the world. Unfortunately, many believers say "yes" to Jesus but don't live in the promise. If we don't take full advantage of the gift of salvation while we're here on earth, then the gospel is only "kind of" good news—the *someday* kind.

JOY BRINGER CHALLENGE

I challenge you to take a deep look into your heart and identify any areas in your life where you may not have fully trusted in God's promise or withheld areas of your heart and life from the Lord. Are there areas where you have looked to other things to bring you joy? Ask the Lord to reveal to you the areas he wants to light up with his love and his true joy. The first part of Proverbs 16:20 says, "Those who listen to instruction will prosper." So, let's begin by asking the Lord for instruction and listening to his voice.

Pray with me:

Lord, thank you for your great love. Thank you for all you've done for me. I want to know you more; I want to trust you more. I want all that you have for me. Will you reveal the areas where I have not fully allowed myself to trust you? Will you show me the areas you want to flood with your love and joy?

Write down what he says. And don't worry if you struggle to hear or wonder if it's the voice of the Lord. We'll get there, I promise. Just write down the things that come to mind.

_____

_____

_____

_____

_____

_____

_____

_____

_____

_____

_____

Thank you, Lord. I trust that you have great intentions for me on this journey. I will listen to your voice and I know that you are faithful to fill me with joy.

Chapter 3:

The Original Joy Bringer

Joy verse

But the angel said to them, "Do not be afraid. I bring you good news that will cause great joy for all the people."–Luke 2:10 NIV

Isn't it exciting to find out that your favorite book is going to be made into a movie? Finally everyone will know why you love the story so much. But then the dread sets in. What if they don't do it justice? What if they use an actor who's nothing like the way you imagine the lead character? There are many reasons for casting choices, but no one thinks to ask you!

Reading the book is almost always better than watching the movie. The world you envision in your mind is so intimate and personal, and like a dream, hard to explain. I can imagine the pressure when a casting director gets a call from a producer who says, "We are making a film of the Bible. We need you to find us the perfect Jesus." Ha! No pressure there! Jesus is only the most personal, controversial, and complex person in history! Not a job I'd want, that's for sure.

The thing that bothers me the most is that Jesus is rarely depicted as joyful. Don't misunderstand me. I don't need Jesus to be a bouncy extrovert, but I would like to see another side of Jesus brought to life on the big screen. One of the biggest misconceptions about him is that he was a quiet wallflower who just wanted everyone to get along. But actually, Jesus was a powerful, charismatic man who—from the moment he arrived on the scene—was a Joy Bringer.

Jesus is our salvation. Jesus is our joy. When we say "yes" to the love and forgiveness of Jesus, the invitation is to follow him, to be more like him. In order to do that, we need to get to know him.

Hebrews 1:9 says of Jesus, "You love justice and hate evil. Therefore, O God, your God has anointed you, pouring out the oil of joy on you more than on anyone else." Did you catch that? Jesus has more joy than anyone at any time in the whole universe! Being born again into a new life, becoming a new creation in Christ means that means we get access to his joy.

Bundle of Joy

JOYFUL DISCOVERY

Did you know that babies can feel joy even in the womb? When Mary found out she was pregnant, she ran away to her cousin Elizabeth's house to find comfort and safety. Elizabeth, who was significantly older than Mary, was also pregnant. Scripture tells us in Luke chapter 1, that at the very greeting of Mary at her door, Elizabeth's baby leapt with joy in her womb. The tiny baby Jesus, who wasn't even past the first trimester of his development, carried the fullness of the Spirit. Mary's baby inside of her released joy and the power of the

Holy Spirit to people she came in contact with. He was a Joy Bringer before he was even breathing air!

There are many ways to announce the birth of a child, just consult Pinterest. But, none of them are as epic as an angel with a trumpet (backed up by an equally epic heavenly choir) declaring that your baby is the long-awaited good news of great joy for all people (Luke 2:10)! Jesus was a Joy Bringer in the womb, at first breath, and he didn't stop there.

While we don't know too much about his early life, we do have a story that shows that Jesus was "that kind of kid." After a long day of journeying back to their hometown from Jerusalem, Mary discovered that their twelve-year-old son, Jesus, was not with them. They had left him behind! Oh, the horror! After searching for him for *three* days they found him back in Jerusalem in the synagogue talking with the religious leaders and teachers. He wasn't lost, he was perfectly fine. He'd been with them the whole time, captivating them with his knowledge and understanding of the scriptures. I can see it now: the old men and younger hotshot students all smiling, laughing, and in awe of this young man who astonished them and brought joy to their hearts. He was refreshing, and probably the talk of the synagogue for a long time.

The Other Side of The Tracks

When news began to spread that Jesus of Nazareth was the promised one, the mere mention of his name caused doubt. "Jesus of...*Nazareth*? Can *anything* good come from *there*?" It didn't look good. Jesus was born to an *unmarried virgin*, he was adopted, grew up in a town that was not on the list of best places to live, and his family line was full of drama—from prostitutes and scary uncles to rich men and great Kings.

There is a long history in our world of success being tied to family, wealth, and location. It makes sense that a governor's son would have the best education and all the opportunities he would need to then become a successful politician himself. Or a beautiful actress marries a talented singer, they have a baby who then has super genes and also becomes a mega-talented performer (and it helps to carry the name for recognition).

In this world of wealth begets wealth, and fame begets fame, do you feel like you're out of luck? Do people see you and your family and think you could never have success or change the patterns of poverty, lack, and unfulfilled dreams? You're not alone, they thought the same thing about Jesus.

If Jesus and his family line was chosen to fulfill the promise and bring joy to the world, then no matter where you are from, what your family has gone through, or what patterns your life has repeated, good can come from you! You can be a Joy Bringer, just like Jesus. This is why I am so glad you are on this journey with me.

Joyful Miracles

One would think that the first public miracle Jesus would perform would be a dramatic healing or another parting of the waters—something of biblical proportions. But just like his birth brought joy to the world, Jesus's first miracle brought joy to the party. It went something like this:

> It wasn't over. They still had days left. But to the horror of the hosts, the wine was about to run out. It was understood that when the wine ran out the party was over, and in this case, shame would be heaped on the host family. Mary pulls her son aside and tells him, "Jesus, they have no more wine." Did she know? Had he done it before? What was the wine

supply like in their home? Jesus replied, "It's not really our business, mom. And it's not my time yet." Mary, a faith-filled woman and mom, grabs the nearest servant and says, "Do what he tells you to do." She knew her son—she believed in him. After a few simple instructions to the help, what could have been a disaster became a new infusion of joy. The wine was not only flowing and in no danger of running out—it was the best they'd ever tasted! You can just about feel the pride and love in Mary's heart and hear the thoughts in her head. Most likely her thoughts were, "That's my son."

Contrary to history's portrayal, Jesus was full of life and joy. The fact that he chose to display his power and authority to enhance a party shows that he was, and is, serious about joy. Biblically, wine is a symbol of joy and happiness. To us, it seems almost insignificant that he turned water into wine. We are more intrigued with his work healing the sick and raising the dead. But this act of love and kindness isn't any different! Why do we tend to put a hierarchy on some miracles and not others?

The breakthrough of joy and peace is just as life-giving and powerful as restoring health to a sick person or the provision of something when there was nothing. We have come into agreement with the lie that the forgiveness of murder and corruption is bigger than the forgiveness of gossip and laziness. The concept is the same. The power of love is the same across the board and we can't live without it. We are desperate for a touch from God.

The restoration of our joy is just as important to the Lord as anything else. We place the restriction and hierarchy on the Lord. It's time we recognize and receive all He has for us. The truth is Jesus did do a miracle of biblical proportions on that day. He revealed his plan to bring unlimited joy and peace to the world forever.

Walking Good News

Jesus walked in two realities. He simultaneously lived on this earth but existed in the Kingdom of God. In fact, he came to bring that Kingdom to earth. Again and again he would say, "It's here!" The Kingdom of heaven is here now because Jesus is with us, here and now. That's why Jesus would tell stories about what the kingdom of God is like, so we could begin to understand and live in its freedom and power. Jesus wanted his disciples (and us) to boldly live as children of God and to understand what that means for us. Jesus, the son of God, lived with confidence in his Father. He walked with authority because he knew who his Father was. Jesus declared that everything he said or did was out of a passionate and powerful relationship with his Father. They were one. And because of Jesus, we can be one too!

Why was Jesus a man of such great joy? Because of the intimacy he had with his Father. He knew total satisfaction and the fulfilment of perfect love. He never sinned because he never lacked anything. He had access to everything he needed because of his complete faith in his Father to provide it for him. Jesus never worried about lack because he didn't experience it! What looked to others like lack was only an opportunity for provision and abundance. The Son of God knew such pure love and fullness of joy that there was never a need to strive or seek. He was the perfect example of what it looked like to live a life connected to and reliant on the Father.

Psalm 16:11 says, "You will make known to me the path of life; In Your presence is fullness of joy; In Your right hand there are pleasures forever." Jesus said of himself, "I am the way, the truth and the life" (John 14:6). He led the way. He lived his life as a perfect example. He knew the fullness of joy because he was in perfect unity with the Father. Do you want to know what is found in the presence of God? The fullness of joy and great pleasures! I want that, don't you? Jesus said we can have that if we follow him. He walked and talked good news! What joy!

Offensive Joy

Jesus brought joy everywhere he went but that didn't mean everyone was happy about it. Joy can be very disruptive and even offensive. When he showed up to difficult and painful situations things changed. He met strife and chaos with peace, hate and ridicule with love. He met injustice, bondage, and pain with healing, restoration, and upgrade! When people encountered Jesus they left changed, never to be the same. From outcast to chosen, isolated to bonded in family, Jesus even changed names to double down on his point—marked, different, changed! He saw the truth from heaven's perspective and when he revealed it, it produced joy in (most) people. Those he touched were filled with joy, and his enemies hated it.

Getting to know Jesus as a Joy Bringer helps make the case that joy is indeed for us. The enemy doesn't want us to live in the fullness of our salvation and he certainly doesn't want us to be like Jesus. Because of fear many of us are afraid of the unknown, therefore we hold on to what we do know, even if it is harmful. We believe the lie that joy is only for certain people, and we miss out on the joyful gospel.

I spent many years being a part of an emotional healing ministry called Freedom Prayer. At the end of one session the woman I was praying with said, "Okay, I have to confess something to you." I was intrigued. This is what she said:

> *"The first time I saw you up on the platform at church,*
> *I did not like you at all. I thought to myself, 'Ugh! Of all the*

people at this church she is the last person I would ever want to be stuck in a room with.' There was something about you that I just didn't like. Then as I pulled up to church for my session, I saw you standing there waiting for me and thought, 'Oh Lord! Anyone but her!' But I knew that the Lord had a plan, so I got out of the car. You were nice and friendly, but I was very uncomfortable. As you prayed over me and we began, I let go and opened myself up to receive what the Lord was going to do through you. And now, everything is different! I know now why I felt that way the first time I saw you. The enemy was telling me, 'See that girl up there? See the joy she has? You'll never have that.' I believed the voice of the enemy telling me that I would never have the joy and freedom that you have, but that's a lie! I feel it! I know it's for me! I am sorry that I judged you that way, but I am so glad that you have the courage to stand up in front of so many people every week and show them what joy and freedom look like."

Becoming more like Jesus means receiving the joy of our salvation. When we receive it, it shines through us and into the world. Like Jesus, as we encounter people, we have the power to leave a wake of joy. Yes, there will be some who don't like it. You may be minimized, overlooked, or even ridiculed for your joy. It may seem personal, but it's not. They don't understand. In one way or another, they've been convinced that joy isn't for them. But like the woman I prayed for, when there is a real touch from the Lord, things change. Joy disrupts the enemy's plan to keep us down, small, and burdened.

Jesus's life wasn't just to be recorded in a book and observed for historical reasons. His life was intended to be an example for us. God's plan isn't a secret. He revealed his desire for us to follow

The Way (Jesus Christ) and experience the fullness of joy (Psalm 16:11). The Lord made good on that promise and revealed the path—it's Jesus! His presence *is* the fullness of joy. God is serious about abundance and love. The enemy is serious about stealing, killing, and destroying all of the goodness. The path of life doesn't just include joy—it's powered by it! No matter what the movies portray, or the historians have focused on, Jesus was a man of great joy, and he brought that joy to the world and to you.

JOY BRINGER CHALLENGE

In your experience, how have you thought of and related to Jesus? What's he been like to you as you've read scripture, seen movies, or had spiritual encounters? Below in the box, write the words that you have used to describe him. Example: Savior, teacher, friend, master, stranger, historical figure. There aren't any wrong words.

As you've thought about the ways in which you've related to Jesus and written them in the box, I challenge you to allow Jesus to expand your box. His greatest desire is to grow in an intimate relationship with you, knowing him in a deeper way. Breaking Jesus out of the neat and safe box we've created for him can be scary, but as we've learned, Jesus is a Joy Bringer, and we can trust that his intention is to lead us into a fullness of joy. Will you pray and declare this with me?

> *Jesus, thank you for who you have been to me. And thank you for your generous invitation to get to know you more. I'm grateful that no matter how many ways I describe you or experience you I can never get to the end of your goodness. You are always inviting me into a new, fresh and beautiful revelation of who you are. While I may be nervous, I declare that your intention is to bring me more joy. So, I thank you for who you've been to me and I ask you to reveal who you would like to be to me in this season. I want to take you out of my box and know you even more. Thank you for loving me. I trust you.*

If the Lord revealed to you who he would like to be to you in this new season, write it down. Dive into scripture and study that quality or characteristic. For years I related to him as my big, sexy husband, Jesus. I understand that that description may be offensive to you. I was coming out of an extremely abusive marriage, and he wanted to show me what it meant to be loved, cherished, protected, and cared for as a bride. He wanted me to know pure love and it was incredible. Then Jesus invited me to let him be my best friend. Best friend, Jesus. It was different and so fulfilling! Our relationship became more fun, with constant companionship and joy! Currently, I am in a season of connecting with Jesus as my source and confidence. When the time is right, I know I will be invited to experience him in a new way that will add even more depth and understanding of him and I welcome it!

Jesus wants to bring you so much joy! It's who he is. I bless you to receive it!

Chapter 4:

The Joyful Cross

Joy verse

"The women ran quickly from the tomb. They were very frightened but also filled with great joy, and they rushed to give the disciples the angel's message."—Matthew 28:8 NLT

My husband and I spent our honeymoon touring around the massive cathedrals of Rome. I couldn't help but be struck by the various artistic, ornately detailed depictions of the crucifix: Jesus hanging on the cross, wearing only a loin cloth and a crown of thorns, drops of sweat and blood on his brow and, according to some artist's interpretations, his gaze set up to the heavens. There certainly isn't anything joyful about that moment. Or is there?

How is it that something so painful, lonely, unfair, and ancient, also holds the distinction of being the most freeing, eternal, joyful, personal, and powerful act in all the world? The answer is because it was thought up and accomplished by Jesus, the son of God, even before the foundation of the world. A supernatural marvel that deserves our attention and effort to understand. What happened that day on a hill just outside the walls of Jerusalem isn't just an ancient act or artistic expression. Jesus's death on the cross was the emancipation of our souls. In that very moment, we were granted freedom from the bondage of our sin. We were absolved from the guilty verdict and punishment we deserve. Because of his pain and suffering we were given full access to be in a loving and eternal relationship with the Father in heaven. The moment Jesus took on the weight and punishment of all the sin of all the world for all time, we were given a choice—the choice to receive that freedom or reject it.

But wait, there's more!

A few years ago, we made the decision to get rid of cable TV. But do you know what I secretly miss about it? The guilty pleasure of the late-night infomercial. Knives, workout equipment, pillows, cooking tools, cleaning agents—you name it. After a solid half hour, my half open eyes and sleepy brain would get sucked in and I would seriously consider reaching for my wallet (and did, more times than I care to admit!). While the products varied, the one thing they all had in common was the deal. "But wait! There's more!" A phrase that gets us every time! Who doesn't want more? Two for the price of one, plus all the extras? Sign me up!

Contrary to popular opinion, being saved isn't about fire insurance (being saved from hell). If the only reason to say yes to a relationship with Jesus was to go to heaven, then why wouldn't we be immediately whisked away to heaven the instant we said yes? Eternity is a part of the promise, but if we stop there we miss out on the good stuff! We get to keep unpacking the gift. The package also includes freedom from the weight of our sin. When we are forgiven, we are also absolved from the shame that sin carries. But wait! There's more! Not only do we get forgiveness, absolution of the punishment of our sin, but we also get the blessing of His love and presence! In exchange for our sin, we are given freedom, and freedom is where we find joy. Our God really is a God of abundance!

I've heard it said that we aren't saved *from* hell, we are saved *for* a relationship with the Lord. Jesus made that possible. He has paid the price of our sin. He has closed the gap of distance between us and our Holy, Awesome God. Because of his death we no longer need elaborate ritual and sacrifice. The cross restored our connection so that we, once again, can live in intimacy with the Father. Jesus is our way back to the Garden of Eden. He fulfilled the plan and promise.

While the experience of the cross wasn't happy, the effects of the cross are joyful. Believe it or not, joy was actually present during the excruciating experience. Scripture tells us that it was the joy set before Jesus that allowed him to endure the cross. Joy! It was the joy of a future relationship with you and me that helped him through it. As he was tortured and left for dead, he focused his thoughts on us. He dreamt of what it would be like to walk, talk, dream, laugh, and love *you*. He thought of how you and I will change the world. He breathed through the pain as his heart beat for your children and grandchildren. His view of the Kingdom of God looked better with you in it, so he set his eyes to see only the joy of the future.

Suddenly, that brutal depiction of a man suffering and dying on a cross looks different. The strange practice of Christians wearing a mini torture device around their necks or hanging them in their homes doesn't seem as dark. What is really being celebrated is the freedom and joy we have because of Jesus's experience on the cross. The cross of pain, shame, fear, and death becomes a symbol of freedom, intimate relationship, and joy.

That joyful morning

For those of us who have grown up around the church, we are accustomed to celebrating (if you can call it that) Good Friday. It's a bizarre name for a day that commemorates the day Jesus was crucified and died, but the reason it can have that name is because He's alive! The Good Friday experience points to the celebration that happens on Easter Sunday. That morning, heaven looked death in the face and laughed. That morning, mourning turned into dancing. That morning, our lives were granted eternal hope and joy forever. That morning, we were given purpose and power to go and tell the good news.

Joyful story

They hadn't slept. They hadn't stopped crying. They couldn't wait for the sun to rise. His death on the cross was the most brutal ending to the longest, most helpless day. Carrying his body to the tomb and laying him in it was the hardest thing they had ever done. How could he be gone? How could this be over? He had changed their lives in ways that never seemed possible and now he was gone. Going back home didn't seem right. How could they just leave him there? But they chose obedience—to honor the Sabbath. Headed back home at sundown on Friday they couldn't wait to return at sunrise on Sunday to honor him properly. Before it began, they ran to the marketplace to purchase spices to be ready to leave at the crack of dawn on Sunday. The hours ticked by so slowly.

They didn't sleep—only waited until the first light. As the sun began to rise, they grabbed their spices and practically ran to the tomb. The only thing that might possibly help them feel better was to anoint him and honor him in death as he had

honored them in life. It was the best and least they could do.
They felt so helpless.

    As they arrived, their anticipation turned to fear. Why was
the stone rolled away? Had someone taken him? Hadn't they
suffered enough?! As they cautiously approached the opening,
they were met by a man who seemed to be glowing. He told
them that Jesus—their Jesus—was alive. His message didn't
seem possible but, then again, they had seen him bring others
back from the dead. Couldn't he do it for himself? Suddenly
they were filled with hope. Adrenaline pumping through their
veins, they began to run. This time their running was pur-
poseful. They were running toward life, not death, propelled
by joy. Their only goal was to tell everyone Jesus is alive!

Like the women who encountered the risen Jesus, when we
encounter the power of the living God everything shifts. Like the
rising of the sun, the risen Son shines the light of his love into our
darkness. We go from wandering lost and hopeless, to on mission,
full of confidence, joy and power. The enemy wants people to
doubt the work of Jesus on the cross and the power of His resurrection. If it wasn't real, then we would have no reason to hope.
But it was real, and the power is still in effect today.

Before Barack Obama ran for the office of the President of the
United States, he wrote a book titled, *The Audacity of Hope*. What
a title! I believe that the resurrection of Jesus from the dead is the
power for us to have audacious, crazy, bold, and powerful hope.
Hope that Jesus is who he says he is. Hope that he will do what he
said he would. Hope in the things unseen and hope in the future.

Do you know what the enemy hates even more than our hope?
The joy it produces! Proverbs 10:28 says, "The hope of the righteous brings joy, but the expectation of the wicked will perish"

(ESV). This is great news because our hope and joy isn't rooted in our ability to perform. We can't earn our hope or work for our joy. Our hope is in the faithfulness of God and our joy is in Jesus.

I love the definition of hope found in the Amplified Bible translation (2 Corinthians 1:7 AMP), "The joyful anticipation of good." Bill Johnson explains that hope gives us the opportunity to experience and enjoy the emotional benefit of a miracle or victory before it happens. What's more powerful than a child of God walking through the difficulty and destruction in the world with a deep hope in the faithfulness and goodness of God, filled with constant and real joy? Nothing! If you have already placed your faith in Jesus, this is a good reminder that God wants you to get your hopes up. He is worthy of your full trust, and you are worthy to receive his joy. If you have not said yes to the offer of salvation, I want to give you that opportunity right now. If you have already surrendered your life to Jesus, I want to help polish up your hope.

JOY BRINGER CHALLENGE

PART ONE

Forgiveness, love, abundant life, and an eternal future is made possible through Jesus. There is nothing more to it than just believing and saying to the Lord something like this:

God, I believe in you. I believe that your son Jesus died for my sins and rose again. I ask you to forgive me and come into my heart and life so that I may know you more. Thank you for loving me.

Congratulations! It's a new day for you, one full of joy and celebration. Scripture says that when one person believes, there is a party thrown in heaven. They are having a joyful celebration over you right now…But I want to celebrate too! If you said yes to Jesus today, will you let me know? Please reach out to me on my website or through social media. That would bring me great joy.

PART TWO

One of the things that works to tarnish our hope, to keep it from sparkling is disappointment. When our expectations are not met, we are often left with pain and questions. No matter how much of a brave face you put on, if you don't deal with the disappointment it will build up and take its toll on your future hopes and expectations. Instead of believing for the good or even the best outcomes we begin to let pessimism and even cynicism function as our protectors, holding hope at arm's length.

Did you know you can be disappointed with God? Often, we are too afraid to admit that we have deep disappointment in the Lord so we hide it. I have been there. I never wanted to admit it because it felt like a sin. I knew God didn't do anything wrong, but I didn't know what to do with my feelings. A trusted pastor lovingly called my attention to it and encouraged me to share my raw feelings with the Lord. I am so glad I did!

I challenge you to search your heart. Allow the God of hope meet you in your disappointment. Tell him how you feel and let him shine his light and love on you to restore your hope in his goodness and fill you with joy.

Chapter 5:

Joyful Inheritance

Joy verse

"You believe in him and are filled with an inexpressible and glorious joy, for you are receiving the end result of your faith, the salvation of your souls." —1 Peter 1:8-9 NIV

I love stories about people who come into an inheritance that they never knew was assigned to them. There is something so romantic about the possibility of getting a phone call from a lawyer that says,

"I am sorry to inform you that your Great-Aunt Sally has died."

"Oh, how sad! Wait...I had a Great-Aunt Sally?!"

"Yes, and because you are named as a beneficiary, you will need to come into my office for the reading of the will."

Millions of dollars later, you are thanking the Lord for your Great-Aunt Sally and the inheritance you didn't know she left you!

My real-life experience with inheritance has been much less romantic, sometimes comical, often complicated, and very painful. My mother loved wiener dogs. We had two. She also collected checkerboards—kitschy themed checkerboards that were usually found in a mountain town country store or antique mall. Her collection included endless options for fun on boards in the shape of barnyard animals, fruit, flags, a schoolhouse, and anything else that could be carved and painted. As her battle with cancer was ending, she wanted to make sure her business was in order. I will never forget the conversation when she informed me that I was not only going to be inheriting the wiener dogs, but yes, the checker-boards too! It certainly was not nearly as exciting or romantic as the fictional Aunt Sally inheritance.

Issues with inheritance can be painful and frustrating. Reading about it may trigger thoughts of anger and even trauma. I understand on a deep level. Or, you may be thinking, "I don't have any wealthy relatives so that leaves me out of a future inheritance." Whether you don't have any inheritance prospects or have been hurt by your experience, the bible brings us good news. "Your hearts can soar with joyful gratitude when you think of how God made you worthy to receive the glorious inheritance freely given to us by living in the light" Colossians 1:12 (TPT).

The Lord loves to join people together in love. The Bible is full of powerful adoption stories and analogies that prove that what was once meant for only the Israelites, is now available for the rest of the world because of what Jesus did through his death on the cross. It was His love for us that moved Him to make a way for everyone to have hope and experience freedom from sin and death. The formal term for what I am referring to is being a joint or co-heir with Christ. What that means is because of what Jesus did, we all, no matter where we come from or what we have done, are now considered children of God. We get to fully receive what is rightfully ours as sons and daughters of the King.

Do you understand what that means? It means that we have a giant pot of all the golden goodness of Heaven with our name written on it. When you said yes to a relationship with God through Jesus Christ His son, you were welcomed into the family of God and put as a beneficiary in the metaphorical will of the Lord! We get what Jesus gets: full access to the Father, the abundance of heaven, and the gifts and fruit of the Holy Spirit.

But wait, there's more, remember? The best news is that you don't have to wait to get to heaven to cash it in. The freedom, goodness, promises, and life-changing love of God, combined with the power that comes from the presence of the Holy Spirit flowing in and through you, is real and it's for you, *right now*. We no longer stand at the back of the line, or hope we know someone who can get us the goods, we get to have full and immediate access to the King! Jesus has made the way so that we can be free from the pain of the past and filled to overflowing with joy. In the next chapter and in the upcoming sections we will dive into the how, but right now I want you to really understand that joy is for you.

Don't eat yellow paint

Vincent van Gogh is known as one of the most famous and important artists in history. In just over a decade, he created over 2100 pieces of art! His life was marked by difficulty and pain. He struggled with depression and anxiety, even psychotic episodes, one that led him to cut off his own ear. He tried many things to help him feel better, including spending time as a missionary, but painting was his passion. Toward the end of his life, his style became bolder and more colorful. As a part of his love and devotion to the Lord, he filled his paintings with yellow. He believed it represented the glory of God and that yellow was the color of joy. As he suffered through depression and anxiety, rumor has it that while in a mental institution he began to eat yellow paint. It is said that he thought it would help his insides become more joyful, coated in joy.

Don't eat yellow paint!

Okay, I know you won't, but the truth is that most of us spend a lot of time and effort, even money, looking for the things that bring us joy. We consume all manner of things to get our fix of joy. And do you know what we come up with? Fleeting moments of happiness that end and leave us unsatisfied. But it isn't necessary! We have abundant and never-ending joy waiting for us to receive, but too often we believe the lies that joy isn't for us. So, we let it sit there and try to fill the void with something else.

Joy is your inheritance. It's free with your "yes" and carries the strength to accomplish more than you know. The Word of God presents thousands of promises, and Proverbs 16:20 is one of them, "Those who trust in the Lord *will be joyful*" (emphasis added). When you received Jesus and were "born again," you came into an inheritance that includes an abundance of joy. 1 Peter 2:8-9 says, "You believe in him and are filled with an inexpressible and glorious joy, for you are receiving the end result of your faith, the salvation of your souls." Peter makes a very presumptuous statement! You believe so, therefore, you are filled with inexpressible and glorious joy. Can you agree to that? Is your joy inexpressible and glorious? That's a pretty big statement. Why was he so bold in saying so?

Peter lived with Jesus. He knew firsthand what it felt like to *walk with Jesus*. In fact, Jesus even re-named him. Talk about being born again! He understood that new life in Jesus and joy go hand in hand. His personal experience was so powerful that he was able to confidently make such a bold statement. To him, it wasn't a crazy assumption or fantasy. He knew without a doubt that being born again led to inexpressible and glorious joy.

Peter goes on to say that joy comes from receiving the end result of your faith which is the salvation (read freedom, wholeness, healing, joy, and the hope of eternity) of your souls, right now. You don't have to wait to get to heaven to get the good stuff. It's your re-birth right. If you are born again, you get it now. Freedom from the bondage of sin and the power and presence of the living God inside of you brings inexpressible joy. If you don't claim that inheritance it's like there is a big ol' bottomless pot of gold in your living room, that has your name on it, comes tax free, and you don't have to do anything else to get it, yet you don't take it to the bank!

Even if we say we know we can have joy, many of us live without it. The enemy wants to try and disqualify or exempt you from your inheritance. There are many lies and misconceptions that he'd have you believe. Here is a list of common reasons I often come across. There may be more, but this is intended to help you identify where you are so we can move forward in truth and great expectation.

- Joy is for extroverts and perky people, it's just not my personality type.
- Joy is not a strong quality.
- My life is too stressful to be joyful.
- I'll have joy when: my wayward child comes home, my spouse comes to know the Lord, my illness is healed, I can pay my bills, etc.
- Joy isn't taken seriously and in order to be in my position I need to be respected.
- Joy is not necessary to be a Christian.
- Leadership is a serious burden, there is no room for joy.
- Joy is too emotional or feminine.
- I've experienced too much pain to have joy in my life.

- My past is full of bad things, God is too mad at/disappointed with me to give me joy.

No matter what the enemy has tried to get you to believe, by now you know that it's not about him, it's all about Jesus. You don't need to be perky, or an extrovert, or have a perfect life to have joy. It is not dependent on your personality or your circumstances. Joy is for you. Joy is for you because Jesus is for you. Say it, *JOY IS FOR ME.*

JOY BRINGER CHALLENGE

I challenge you to get to the bottom of why you may believe you are disqualified from joy. When you're ready, read the following prayer, and be ready to listen and write down what you hear:

Thank you, God, for who you are. Thank you for loving me and wanting me to live in the fullness of my salvation. I believe joy is for me because you are for me. Lord, please bring to mind any lies I have believed and agreements that I have made that are contrary to your Word and the promises you have for me. I am listening and I know that you are gracious to meet me in this moment.

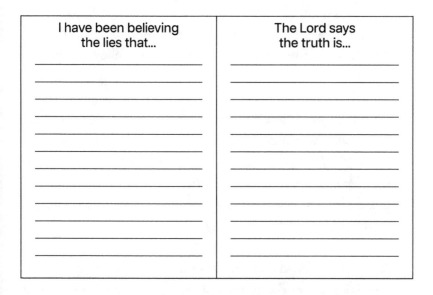

I have been believing the lies that...	The Lord says the truth is...

Now that you are aware of the lies you have been believing and the agreements you've made about joy, let's ask the Lord what is true. He loves the truth! He *is* truth, and he *loves* when we seek it. Pray with me:

> *Thank you, Lord, for revealing these things to me. I trust that they were revealed to me in order for you to replace my beliefs with your truth. Thank you for never leading us into pain or traumatizing us. I am asking you to replace each lie I have listed with the truth. I want to know what YOU have to say about me and what I have been believing. I trust you, Lord. I am ready to receive what you have for me.*

Read each lie or agreement you wrote down and ask, "Is this the truth, Lord?" Wait for his answer and then ask, "What is the truth you want me to believe?" and write that down next to the lie.

Were you surprised by what the Lord said? If what you have been believing about joy isn't true according to the voice of the

Lord, are you willing to surrender the lie and come into agreement with the truth? I hope so! Now you can follow it up with this prayer:

> *Thank you, Lord, for the truth. Thank you that your love is far greater than I understand. Help me to see you and your desire for my life more clearly. I repent for believing the lies about myself. I want to live fully in your truth. I want to experience the abundant life you have for me. I love you, Lord, and I thank you for loving me.*

No matter what the enemy has said, or what you have been told, joy is a result of the overwhelming love of God. If you have a tough time grabbing hold of that, you're not alone. It's really *that* big and *that* crazy. It should blow your mind. God's love for you is far beyond our understanding, but that does not mean we should write it off. We need to press into it. There is so much to learn from God's love for us and others and it deserves our attention.

Chapter 6:

Joy Bringer's Core Value—Gratitude

Joy verse

"Always be joyful. Never stop praying. Be thankful in all circumstances, for this is God's will for you who belong to Christ Jesus." –1 Thessalonians 5:16-18 NLT

Throughout this section I have tried to establish the importance of joy in the life of a Jesus follower. Jesus not only lived as a Joy Bringer, he wants you to as well. And although we've discussed some of the ways you can take hold of that joyful inheritance Jesus offers, you may be wondering, "But *how*?!" Great question! We've come to our first Joy Bringer's Core Value!

These are meant to give you something to hold onto—joy handles, if you will—to grab hold when life happens, and the enemy tries to steal your joy. I want to equip you with the tools to choose joy and maintain it. It's always available for us, but it isn't always what our flesh wants to agree with. Sometimes it's downright hard to choose. These core values are tested and true. They have seen me through the most difficult and tragic circumstances. They are simple and doable. They will help you in times of doubt, sadness, confusion, fear, tragedy, and anything else that can get in the way of joy filling you and flowing out.

The first Joy Bringer's Core Value is Gratitude. It's our response to the incredible gift of salvation through Jesus, the foundation of our joy.

The Glad Game

When I was little, I loved Shirley Temple and Hayley Mills. They were cute, talented, and their movies were played on repeat in my home. One of my favorites was the movie, *Pollyanna*. She was an orphan who was sent off to live with her rich Aunt Polly. In classic Disney movie fashion, Pollyanna's outlook on life and joyful spirit transforms the dreary town and everyone she encounters is changed for the better.

One of the things Pollyanna was known for was the glad game. Her father was a minister and they had very little money and resources. Often, they would ask the missionary organization to send a missionary barrel—donations of clothes, toys, and other useful items. The glad game was created when her excited, expectant family would open the barrels to find less than desirable items. Specifically, when Pollyanna wanted a doll more than anything and instead inside the barrel was a pair of crutches. While it was hard to find a reason to be glad about receiving crutches instead of a doll, they decided that they were glad they didn't have cause to use them!

Choosing to find the good and be grateful in difficult circumstances is vital to living a life full of joy. Notice I said vital, not easy. It's not always easy to come into agreement with gratitude. Pollyanna has gotten a bad rap. In fact, her name is used to accuse someone of being silly, too hopeful, or not facing real issues with grit. But that's where the breakdown happens. Pollyanna was incredibly strong! She was a young woman with great difficulty in her life. An orphan, sent to live with a dowager old woman. Surrounded by grumpy and hopeless people, she could have easily agreed with the hopelessness around her, but she didn't. She saw the circumstances and yet chose to deal with the difficulty by being grateful. She wasn't running from the problems, she took up her weapon of gratitude, fought the battle and won! The whole community was changed because of her choice to be grateful and choose joy.

Joy thief

Theodore Roosevelt said, "Comparison is the thief of joy." And boy was he right! Nothing can discourage us faster than when we begin to compare what we have to what others have. And let's not be fooled, that's the enemy's goal. He *loves* it when we can't receive something wonderful from the Lord because we are too busy eyeing what others have and comparing our portion to those around us. It's a nasty and powerful weapon and most of us have been taken down by it. But oh man, when we pull out our weapon of gratitude and hold onto it, we can fight that attack and win!

Gratitude is the gateway into the Kingdom. By expressing our thanks and appreciation for what we do have, we turn away from lack, fear, comparison, and hopelessness. We say no to the lies the enemy would have us believe and say yes to the truth. God knows our needs and is providing for us. The Lord has a great plan for us to grow and prosper. We have the very real presence and power of the Holy Spirit to comfort, counsel, and guide us. When we begin to state the things we do have and are grateful for, we take on a posture of worship—assigning value to the Lord.

I bet I don't have to tell you that this isn't always easy. Remember Pollyanna? She was a master at choosing to be grateful. But often there is something deep within us that would rather partner with frustration, cynicism, hopelessness, and a "poor me" attitude. I've been there. Sometimes I think I even like the victim role. I want to sit, helpless, and wait for people to feel sorry for me. For many of us it's been our MO (modus operandi, or our preferred way of operating) for a long time. It seems easier to gripe, lash out, and blame than choose gratitude and joy. But we turn once again to the perfect example we have in Jesus. He had all kinds of reasons to be hurt, angry, bitter, and just give up—all the things the enemy would have wanted him to do. But instead, he locked eyes with the Father and gave thanks!

No matter how bad things get, there is always a reason to be grateful. That's why it was necessary to begin this journey by looking at salvation. There are volumes of books on the topic and no possible way to get to the bottom of all that it comes with because it's that big and that good. The foundation of our joy, the source, is Jesus. Because Jesus never changes, our joy never has to change. In him alone there are countless reasons to have great joy.

So, when it comes time to grab hold of the Joy Bringer's Core Value of gratitude and fight against the attacks of the enemy, what do you do if you feel resistance and aren't able to voice your gratitude and appreciation? Start with Jesus. Begin with life. Acknowledge the Lord's presence even if you can't feel it. Remember the past when the Lord rescued you, provided for you, loved you, spoke to you, and how he has changed your life. Say it aloud, "Thank you! Thank you, Lord, for what you've done! Thank you, Lord, for what you are doing right now. Thank you for the grace to feel what I am feeling and the power to choose to fight!" Start there and then keep going. No matter how much resistance you feel, no matter how bad things may look, pick up your weapon of gratitude and choose to fight! Jesus fought for you and because of his love we have victory and joy!

JOY BRINGER CHALLENGE

Let's begin now. I challenge you to write down the things you are grateful for. How has Jesus brought joy to your life? You can start with the big things, or the small things, just begin. Be grateful and let the joy rise up!

_____

_____

_____

_____

_____

_____

_____

_____

_____

_____

Section 2:

Healing

Joy verse:
"News about him spread as far as Syria, and people soon began bringing to him all who were sick. And whatever their sickness or disease, or if they were demon possessed or epileptic or paralyzed—he healed them all."—Matthew 4:24 NLT

Joy Principle:
Everything changes when King Jesus shows up

Joy Bringer's Core Value:
Forgiveness

If you know me, you know my love language is lunch with friends. It's what I do! Great conversation over an iced tea and huge salad brings me life. And straws. Straws are an obsession of mine (the reusable ones, of course). I don't drink anything without a straw, hot or cold. If it's going in my mouth, then it's through a straw. And if you've ever seen me in my car, you will know it's me because of my Joy Bringer sticker. My husband had it made for me as a surprise and because of it, everyone knows it's me on the road.

Knowing someone means you know what makes them who they are. What they love or do are the things that identify them. It would be impossible to say you know me without knowing that I love Jesus or that I am totally addicted to tea. The same applies to Jesus—to know him means to know he's a healer. It's what he does.

Everywhere Jesus went he healed people, and his reputation grew so quickly that people didn't wait for him to come to their city, they would bring the sick to him. And do you know what he did? He healed them. He healed them all. And he wants to heal you too.

> *"Jesus traveled throughout the region of Galilee, teaching in the synagogues and announcing the Good News about the Kingdom. And he healed every kind of disease and illness. News about him spread as far as Syria, and people soon began bringing to him all who were sick. And whatever their sickness or disease, or if they were demon possessed or epileptic or paralyzed—he healed them all."—Matthew 4:23-24.*

Like joy, healing has a bit of a mixed reputation. It can be a very touchy subject. Depending on our experience (or lack thereof), healing can conjure up feelings of immense gratitude and joy but also sadness, anger, bitterness, and confusion. Countless books have been written on the subject and there are people who are specifically anointed to write, speak, and minister on healing. Healing is a huge part of receiving the fullness of the joy of the Lord and bringing it wherever you go. The wounds of our lives have great effect on our joy and it's vital to understand that (just like joy) healing is for you because Jesus is for you—it's what he does.

When we think of healing, most often we associate it with our physical needs. But healing isn't limited to a physical nature. There are many kinds of healing including emotional, spiritual, and the healing of broken and incorrect beliefs. Ultimately, Jesus came to heal the brokenness of humanity and restore us to an intimate and powerful relationship with the Father. That's what Isaiah 53:5 is all about when the scripture says,

> *"But he was pierced for our transgressions,*
> *he was crushed for our iniquities;*
> *the punishment that brought us peace was on him,*
> *and by his wounds we are healed."*

I have experienced powerful healing in my life. I have seen great works of physical healing happen in front of my eyes. I have experienced and been a part of other people's life-changing encounters of emotional healing and spiritual freedom. At the same time, I have struggled with questions, confusion, sadness, and doubt. I have experienced great disappointment, pain, and even anger toward God when there hasn't been healing (on this side of eternity). I have walked alongside others as they have navigated the same struggles. Because of the sensitive nature of this subject many of us have simply chosen to avoid it completely and ride out the pain. But the healer wants to heal that wound too.

There have been horrible things said and done in the name of Jesus that have caused deep pain and wounded many. If you are one of them and are about ready to skip this section or even put this book down for good, please let me say something.

I am deeply sorry.

I am so sorry for the words or actions of others who have taken the powerful gift of healing and used it to bring shame, confusion, or fear into your life. I am sorry for the phrases that have been used like, "You just need more faith" or "You must have some hidden sin in your life making you so ill." Or how about the so-called well-meaning Christian who says, "God must be trying to teach you a lesson" or when someone passed away said, "God must need them more than you do."

My heart breaks for the hope lost and the wedge placed between you and the good and loving healer, Jesus. It is my deepest desire to help to restore truth to the area of healing and help provide some clarity and confidence for you to approach the Lord.

Do you remember the story of the people who carried their paralyzed friend to Jesus on a mat (Luke 5:17-26)? The house was too crowded—they couldn't get close to him. But having their friend encounter the healer was so important to them they decided to make a hole in the roof of the house and lower him down. That was no easy feat! Jesus not only healed the paralyzed man but forgave him of his sin (which made the religious onlookers really mad).

We don't know much about the man on the mat. Was he a skeptic? Had he given up hope? Did he want to meet Jesus but couldn't do it on his own? Either way, praise God for friends with faith, strong backs, and perseverance! It was the faith of the friends that impressed Jesus.

Sometimes we need someone to help carry us. In some way I am holding a corner of your mat. I don't know what your experience with healing has been, whether you have been hurt or disappointed, or whether you are excited to learn more and dive in. Wherever you are, you are not alone on this journey. I am with you. Jesus is with you. You are safe to proceed. The healer is waiting.

Chapter 7:

Physical Healing

Joy verse

He took her by the hand and said to her, "Talitha koum!"
(which means "Little girl, I say to you, get up!")–Mark 5:41 NIV

Not much is worse than when someone you love is suffering. We will do just about anything to help them. Do you remember the story of the man who brought his tormented son to Jesus? The man in his weariness tells Jesus that they have tried everything, and even Jesus' disciples couldn't help him. In a final effort, the man asks Jesus to have mercy on him and help his son. But then he adds "if you can." Let's read about it in Mark 9:22-24. The scripture says:

"What do you mean, 'If I can'?" Jesus asked. "Anything is possible if a person believes."

The father instantly cried out, "I do believe, but help me overcome my unbelief!"

The man looks at Jesus, the son of God in the face and admits that he has doubt and what does Jesus do? He heals the boy. Jesus isn't frustrated or angry at us because of our doubts and weary faith. He doesn't turn his back on us and tell us to come back later after we've grown in our faith or turned our lives around. He is moved with compassion when we approach him. He meets us where we are with the fullness of who he is.

One of my favorite quotes is from a man with a fantastic name, Francis Frangipane. He says, "If there is any area of your life that is not glistening with hope, then somewhere you are under the influence of a lie." The Lord sees our past, our current situation, and our future through the lens of victory. From his perspective, everything—and I mean *everything*—is covered in hope. It glistens with his glory. But if the enemy can use disappointment and pain to blind us from the hope we have, then we begin to believe the lie that God doesn't want to heal us. We think that we have done something wrong, that we aren't good enough, or that it's just not real. Our doubts keep us away from the healer. But the Lord isn't afraid of our doubt and he's willing to show us even still.

See for yourself

You can't really argue with the statement "I was blind, but now I see" (John 9:25). Jesus brought sight to the blind. He also restored hearing and the ability to speak (Mark 7:31-35). Jesus restored limbs (Matthew 12:13). He enabled the lame and par-alyzed to walk (Mark 2:11-12). The famous story of the woman with the issue of blood always gets me. Can't we call it what it was? Twelve years of menstrual hemorrhaging! Oh, the horror! Not to mention the cultural shame and isolation. In the Hebrew culture, sickness and disease made you unclean, relegating you to a life on the outside. Leprosy—essentially a skin eating disease—was not just a disfiguring physical ailment, but one that was seen as a spiritual smite from God. If Jesus had a favorite to heal, I believe it was this one (Luke 17:11-19). There were so many physical healings that the gospel writers used phrases like, "he healed all the sick among them" (Matthew 12:15) and "people throughout the village brought sick family members to Jesus. No matter what their diseases were, the touch of his hand healed every one" (Luke 4:40).

The physical healings Jesus performed were often spectacles and caused a great deal of commotion. Even when he told people to keep it to themselves (Mark 1:41-44) his miraculous power drew great attention and that was the point. He wanted to reveal the truth so people would believe who he was—the long-awaited Messiah, the Son of God—and bring glory to the Father. Jesus healed because of love. He was moved with compassion and mercy. Jesus brought joy through his healing touch.

The accounts of Jesus's ministry reveal that he rarely healed the same way twice. Sometimes he simply spoke, other times he touched. He told the ten lepers to go see the priests. There were times when he used elements like spit, mud, and water. In one account we read that it took a few touches from Jesus to restore sight to a blind man (Mark 8:22-26). We don't fully understand why Jesus used these elements or tactics, but we do know that there were always many layers of meaning to his actions. I want to be clear that there are still many ways Jesus heals. Whether immediate or gradual, through medical assistance or an invisible touch, there is no such thing as a second-class healing. I mean it, and I invite you to read that last sentence again.

Miraculous physical healings happen every day. Even still, there are many skeptics and mockers, and those who would argue that the gift of healing ceased in the first century. Unfortunately, the ministry of healing has been abused for personal gain and show. But, nevertheless, the miraculous power of Jesus Christ the healer is still at work (thank God! Literally). I am astounded by the fact that even through our doubt and disbelief, our mistreatment and abuse, God not only heals but chooses to include us in the process. Remember the man known forever because of his doubt? Doubting Thomas needed to see Jesus for himself, even touch his wounds, and Jesus met him with grace and understanding (John 20:24-29).

Perhaps you have experienced it, or you know someone who has. The cancerous tumor that suddenly disappears. The conception of a baby after years of infertility. Knees, backs, shoulders, necks healed and restored to full mobility. I have seen so much glorious healing that I couldn't deny it even if I tried. And I want to see and experience so much more!

Here's one of the most recent testimonies of God's extravagant healing and goodness. My friend Andrew has had a life full of physical challenges. Due to a weak heart as a child, he underwent over a dozen procedures by the time he was twelve. He suffered from Tourette syndrome, which caused regular ticks throughout his body. And on top of that, he was born without an eardrum, leaving him deaf in his left ear. Andrew is a musician, a prayer warrior, and man of great faith. I've had the privilege of praying for many people alongside him and we've seen the Lord's miraculous healing power. I have always been inspired by Andrew, praying for others when he himself had yet to be healed. He was never discouraged after the countless times people laid hands on him. He continued to believe that he was loved by God and that he would be healed someday. He wanted to hear.

Andrew, his wife, my husband and I went to visit a famous church to attend a healing service. We were so excited believing that Andrew would receive the healing he had hoped for. A little boy who had been born deaf and miraculously healed wanted to pray for Andrew. As the boy was laying hands on him, he felt the

Lord wanted to heal Andrew's Tourette syndrome. Andrew felt a heavy weight lift slowly off his body. He felt so light and peaceful that he had to lay down. He was on the ground for a while as we watched from afar wondering what was going on. When he got up and told us what happened we couldn't believe it! Tourettes was gone. He said for the first time in his life his body was at peace. Incredible! God is so amazing! He wasn't asking to be healed from Tourette Syndrome, but God had another plan.

If you're anything like me you may be wondering, "But what about his ear? That's what he *really* wanted healed!" Andrew kept believing and praying. About five years later (a week ago at the time I'm writing this) while sitting alone in his room Andrew heard a few loud pops. Suddenly, he could hear. Without asking, without anyone around, without fasting and prayer, no drama or spectacle. God moved. Overwhelmed with it all, Andrew is learning to use his ear. He told me it's like not having an arm your whole life and suddenly growing one. An adjustment to be sure but in the learning there is a constant reminder of the goodness and glory of God.

New life

The end. Not my favorite two words. I am not a fan of endings, and I certainly don't like goodbyes. I am more of a "see ya later" person. Confession: I often just leave parties without telling anyone. Yup, I'm that person. I told you I don't like goodbyes. I think it's because I've experienced a lot of death in my family. In fact, I am pretty much the only one left. No matter how well or long a life has been lived, the finality of death has a painful sting for those who are left behind, even if you know they are in heaven.

Conception and birth are often referred to as miracles, and without trying to be irreverent, because of the development of science and medical technology, we know exactly how it all happens. Miracles are events caused by divine intervention where the ordinary operation of nature is overruled. But turning death into life, now that's a miracle. Resurrection is not something we think about in our everyday lives but if we're talking about physical healing, it's just about as extreme as it gets! Jesus not only raised many people from the dead, he experienced it himself, and he's still doing it today!

We don't have the gospel without the resurrection of Jesus. He defeated death and the grave. Our King is not dead, he's alive. And while it shocked the tunics off his disciples, it wasn't actually a secret he was trying to keep! Not only did Jesus try to tell them it would happen on many occasions, he showed off his resurrection power multiple times. Let's read what scripture says about this:

> *Soon afterward Jesus went with his disciples to the village of Nain, and a large crowd followed him. A funeral procession was coming out as he approached the village gate. The young man who had died was a widow's only son, and a large crowd from the village was with her. When the Lord saw her, his heart overflowed with compassion. "Don't cry!" he said. Then he walked over to the coffin and touched it, and the bearers stopped. "Young man," he said, "I tell you, get up." Then the dead boy sat up and began to talk! And Jesus gave him back to his mother. (Luke 7:11-15)*

At a funeral! Can you even imagine?

How about this one? Let's read another scripture:

A messenger arrived from the home of Jairus, the leader of the synagogue. He told him, "Your daughter is dead. There's no use troubling the Teacher now."

But when Jesus heard what had happened, he said to Jairus, "Don't be afraid. Just have faith, and she will be healed"....The house was filled with people weeping and wailing, but he said, "Stop the weeping! She isn't dead; she's only asleep." But the crowd laughed at him because they all knew she had died. Then Jesus took her by the hand and said in a loud voice, "My child, get up!" And at that moment her life returned, and she immediately stood up! Then Jesus told them to give her something to eat. (Luke 8:49-50, 52-54)

Incredible! I love that Jesus is never affected by other's doubts. He has so much power over death that he took his sweet time on the journey to see Lazarus (John 11). While everyone else saw his delay as a lack of care or concern, Jesus had a bigger plan to reveal even more of God's glory. He said to his disciples "Lazarus is dead. And for your sake, I'm glad I wasn't there, because now you have another opportunity to see who I am so that you will learn to trust in me" (John 11:14-15 TPT).

I have an interesting relationship with resurrection. In fact, I'm married to it. My husband died when he was fifteen. While in the hospital for a bicycle injury, both of his lungs collapsed. Nothing worked to get him breathing on his own and his heart stopped. The doctors called it and he was officially dead. As they were cleaning up and moving on, breath suddenly filled his lungs and he was brought back to life!

Waking up after being in an induced coma for a few days, he was having a conversation with his mom and said, "What are these red marks on my chest? Did they use the shockers on me?" "I don't think so honey, I can ask the nurse, but I don't see any red marks." Frustrated after not getting any answers about the red marks (they did not use the defibrillator), he closed his eyes and laid back in his hospital bed and had a vision. He saw two hands come down from heaven and heard a voice say, "This is where I touched you." He knew that he was indeed touched by the resurrection power of the Almighty God.

While my husband's story is powerful and fairly unusual, scripture is clear that we all experience a kind of resurrection from the dead because of Jesus's own experience. Let's see what scripture has to say about this:

> *"But God is so rich in mercy, and he loved us so much that even though we were dead because of our sins, he gave us life when he raised Christ from the dead. (It is only by God's grace that you have been saved!) For he raised us from the dead along with Christ and seated us with him in the heavenly realms because we are united with Christ Jesus. So God can point to us in all future ages as examples of the incredible wealth of his grace and kindness toward us, as shown in all he has done for us who are united with Christ Jesus."—Ephesians 2:4-7)*

> *"This means that anyone who belongs to Christ has become a new person. The old life is gone; a new life has begun!"—2 Corinthians 5:17*

Isn't this great news? The old life marked by death because of our sin is completely gone! Because of God's grace, mercy, and love we have been given a new life. It is an abundant one marked by power, freedom, and joy. Our old ways are no longer needed, we've been upgraded big time!

The tricky thing for many of us is that we easily go back to our old ways. They are familiar to us and therefore we sometimes slip back into those habits quite easily. After Jesus healed the paralyzed man at the pool of Bethesda he said to him, "Look at you now! You're healed! Walk away from your sin so that nothing worse will happen to you" (John 5:14 TPT). While Jesus loves to heal our physical bodies, he wants us to know that the sin that so easily entangles us leads us to trouble. While we have been forgiven, sin still has physical consequences on this earth. But God, because of his kindness, has given us an advocate in the Holy Spirit who is always with us. He helps remind us that those old ways lead to death, and He reminds us we have the power to choose life. We'll dive deeper into that in the next section.

But why?

Jesus wasn't and isn't limited by anything. Remember he was the one who said, "Anything is possible with God." So why isn't everyone healed? How come the prayers for healing and freedom don't always get answered? I wish I could answer this question, not only for you but for myself. I have cried out countless times with a guttural, "Why?!" And of course, the desperate, "Please!" There is so much mystery to the ways of the Lord. We will never know the fullness of why things do or don't happen. Nor will we understand the scope of the plan until we are on the proverbial heavenly balcony looking back down. The Apostle Paul says it like this:

> *"Now we see things imperfectly, like puzzling reflections in a mirror, but then we will see everything with perfect clarity. All that I know now is partial and incomplete, but then I*

will know everything completely, just as God now knows me completely."—1 Corinthians 13:12

Oh, that's going to be a good day! But until then, we're not alone. Right there with us in the middle of the unanswered prayers, pain, and suffering of our circumstances is the very real, loving, and compassionate Jesus. We are never promised perfection, we are promised the perfect one (Jesus). We are not given an easy button; Jesus offers to take our heavy burden. We are not always saved from the fire, storm, or war, but we are protected and secure because he is with us.

When there is healing and freedom, gratitude and joy abound. It's cause for celebration. But does that mean that if you're not healed or are still bound then you are disqualified from those things? Well, that is certainly what the enemy wants you to believe! He wants you to think you are alone, you don't deserve to be healed and others have it better than you. He wants you to believe that joy and celebration aren't for you. But here's the profound truth that shatters that lie. Scripture says that in the *presence* of the Lord is found strength and joy (1 Chronicles 16:27). He is with us in the middle of it all. So even if healing doesn't come the way we prayed for, or in our preferred time frame, we still have him. That's cause for gratitude and joy. That's a reason to celebrate.

JOY BRINGER CHALLENGE

Being a Joy Bringer means that we have experienced and received powerful and lasting joy in Jesus. One of the ways we experience it is through his healing touch. If you don't need physical healing right now, you may know someone who does. Because of God's goodness and abundant love, you can be used to bring that joy to someone else. I challenge you:

- If you have a need for physical healing, bring it to Jesus.
- If you know someone who needs physical healing, ask them if you can pray for them. Don't worry, there are no magic words, just ask the Lord to do what he does best.
- Is there is an area of your life that isn't glistening with hope? Perhaps you have been disappointed in the area of physical healing. Ask the Lord to reveal his perspective. He is compassionate and understands your pain.

Chapter 8:

Spiritual Deliverance

Joy verse:
"The light shines in the darkness, and the darkness
has not overcome it."—John 1:5 NIV

There is a huge economic revenue stream from the subject of supernatural, specifically demonic, activity. From books, movies, and TV shows, to businesses, and even board games (the Ouija Board is marketed to children and sold at Target), it's clear that American culture has a fascination with the supernatural. And yet, when it comes to Christians acknowledging the presence or influence of it in our own lives, we often either deny it, ignore it, or are too terrified to even go there.

The spiritual world and those who recognize and operate in it are often placed at the proverbial weirdo table. But it's not weird! In fact, the reality of the spiritual world is confirmed through science. Superstring Theory has proven at least 10 different dimensions giving credence to the experience that many already know to be true. This is not about the existence of extraterrestrials or

Bigfoot, it's about the reality of another realm, one that we may not always see but can often feel and be greatly affected.

A huge part of the gospel accounts of Jesus's ministry and the ministry of the apostles deal with supernatural interference and encounter. Demons, angels, and miracles were a part of everyday life. And, news flash, nothing has changed. Okay, maybe we are more distracted by shiny digital objects (seems pretty strategic to me!) but nevertheless, there are spiritual and supernatural happenings and encounters all around us. It doesn't have to be strange or scary. And we don't have to be weirdos! If we are going to follow Jesus, then we need to not only understand that it's real but something we have power and victory over. We can be naturally supernatural.

Demons in the dark

Spiritual deliverance or freedom can conjure up thoughts of those scary movies where people are possessed and, after a lot of vomit, levitating, and general havoc, the priest is called in for the dramatic battle of good versus evil. But spiritual freedom is far more than the horror movies portray. The spiritual attack of the enemy is waged with bondage and sin.

It's the weight of oppression that we are talking about here, not possession. I do not believe that a person with Christ living inside them can be totally possessed. There is, however, a great oppression that happens when the demonic forces launch an attack. The arrows of the enemy include (but aren't limited to): fear, chaos, lies, deception, confusion, anger, nightmares and strange occurrences. The enemy is crafty and cunning but not creative. When there is a wound, a place of vulnerability, the enemy uses that as a target and launches the same attack at the same place every time. The power and weight of the attack and the pain of the results are so oppressive that it can radically affect people's lives. But then there's Jesus.

> *Then Jesus demanded, "What is your name?"*
> *And he replied, "My name is Legion, because there are*
> *many of us inside this man."—Mark 5:9*

That's no joke! This man who was possessed by a legion of demons was so bound by the enemy's attack that he needed to be physically restricted with chains and separated from society in a cave. He lived like an animal. That's the thing the enemy loves to do—divide and degrade human life. Everyone had written him off. He was a hopeless cause, better off dead (another belief the enemy wants you to agree with). He lived among the tombs, caves of darkness, alone. Darkness is the enemy's playground. Secrets, lies, pain, shame, and fear live in the dark. Then Jesus showed up. The demons didn't stand a chance! When the light of the world shines his love in the dark, the darkness has to go. It's a crazy story that even includes pigs, you should read the whole thing. But Jesus doesn't stop there. Check it out:

> *"Jesus said, 'No, go home to your family, and tell them*
> *everything the Lord has done for you and how merciful he has*
> *been.' So the man started off to visit the Ten Towns of that*
> *region and began to proclaim the great things Jesus had done*
> *for him; and everyone was amazed at what he told them"—*
> *Mark 5:18-20*

His humanity was not just restored, he was given a new identity, purpose, and mission! God's love and goodness is extravagant.

As he destroys the spiritual bondage of our lives, he replaces it with freedom, purpose, and joy.

Evidence of demonic attacks comes in all forms, from extreme cases like we just read to subtle hidden torment or oppression of the mind. One of the most prevalent is fear. When it strikes, it can paralyze us, often rendering us unable to fight. For the most part, fear is a mirage that tricks our minds into working overtime and that causes our bodies to react. Heart palpitations, sweat, shaking, and numbness set in as anxiety takes over our bodies. Once again, the enemy enjoys the abuse of the child of God. 2 Timothy 1:7 shows that fear is spiritual bondage, one that the Lord loves to break and replace. "For God has not given us a spirit of fear, but of power and of love and of a sound mind" (NKJV).

Victory Song

Do you like to win? My competitive side only really appears when playing board games or group competitions—watch out, I'm coming for you. When it comes to the enemy, we don't have to worry about winning because Jesus already won! Because we are in Christ, we have victory too.

> *"My enemies did their best to kill me,*
> *but the Lord rescued me.*
> *The Lord is my strength and my song;*
> *he has given me victory.*
> *Songs of joy and victory are sung in the camp of the godly.*
>
> *The strong right arm of the Lord has done glorious things!"—Psalm 118:13-15*

The enemy wants us to think that it's a close battle, but it's not. We do not need to be afraid of dark demonic attacks because, thanks to the light of Jesus, we have authority. With that said, it is not something we want to play with. The enemy is waiting for us to open doors, giving him permission to come in and wreak havoc. There are some obvious doors like engaging in secret sin, playing with things like Ouija Boards or Tarot cards, but there are also the subtle but effective doors of our ears and eyes.

Our ears and eyes are the only entry points in our lives. What we see and hear has profound effect on our minds, hearts, mouths, and actions. The enemy tempts us to stop and look or listen, to get our attention long enough to slip into our lives. We can protect ourselves by keeping our eyes fixed on Jesus and our ears tuned to his voice. The more we flood our eyes and ears with the love, joy, peace, and goodness of God, the quicker we recognize the efforts of the enemy to change the channel.

I prayed for a woman who was under deep spiritual oppression. Her eyes were sunken in, her hair covered much of her face, and she could barely speak loud enough to be understood. Her past was so traumatic and painful that she was paralyzed in fear. The enemy had his hooks in and honestly there wasn't much life left. As we prayed, everything about her became lighter. She had a powerful encounter with the healing eyes of Jesus. He spoke words of life and it changed her. This woman's eyes were dark brown when we walked in the room, but they were blue when she left! As the power of the enemy was lifted off her, she came alive. She laughed, cried tears of freedom, and we sang together in victory.

Let there be light

Jesus is called "the Word." The first words recorded in the creation story in Genesis 1 are, "let there be light" (Genesis 1:3).

John 1:4-5 says of Jesus, "The Word gave life to everything that was created, and his life brought light to everyone. The light shines in the darkness, and the darkness can never extinguish it." Jesus is the light of the world, but he also calls us the light of the world (Matthew 5:14). He's given us the ability to shine his light and his love everywhere we go. Darkness is only dark because the light hasn't arrived. When light shines, the darkness disappears.

You don't have to be afraid. You have the authority to cast out the demons that want to kill, steal, and destroy your life (Luke 9:1). You don't need someone else to do it. And it doesn't have to be weird. You simply speak to the interference and tell it to go. Remember it was the Word that spoke words of light into the darkness, and it lit up. You also can light up the darkness with words of life and love.

JOY BRINGER CHALLENGE

The Wall: A four-part visual and creative exercise

In order to live lit up with the light of freedom and love, we need to assess if there are any walls blocking the light. We build walls in our hearts, minds, and lives for a few reasons. Because of wounding and sin, we feel a need to hide parts of ourselves, often believing that we would be rejected or ruined if people knew the truth. Pain and fear lead us to build walls of protection keeping people from getting close, keeping ourselves from something that we've deemed dangerous. We can also build walls that keep us from our dreams and purpose. This comes from believing the lies that we are disqualified from an abundant life.

Jesus wants to help us tear down the spiritual and emotional walls and be full of light. But before you begin, I want to remind you that the Lord is infinitely creative. What you see or feel may surprise you and that's OK! We can trust that the Lord knows us better than anyone and can reveal himself and his love for us anyway he likes. We can trust that it's all good.

PART ONE

Ask the Holy Spirit to reveal to you if there is a wall in your life. If so, ask him to show it to you. Write down what you see and keep going!

_____

_____

_____

_____

_____

_____

_____

_____

_____

_____

PART TWO

Ask the Lord the following questions and write down what you hear, if you'd like.

- What is the purpose of the wall?
- When did it get built?
- Who built it?
- What is it made of? (This is where it can get creative and interesting!)
- What is on the other side of the wall? Will you show me?

- Is what's on the other side of the wall something you want for me?
- Is it safe to tear down this wall? (There are times it may not be and that's OK! This is why we are asking the Lord.)
- If it is safe to tear down this wall, what tool will you give me to do so? (This is also a super creative moment!)

_____

_____

_____

_____

_____

_____

_____

_____

_____

_____

PART THREE

If you are ready, tear that wall down! Be aware of the following and write it down if that helps you.

- How do you feel?
- Did it all come down? If not, ask the Lord why.
- Is there any rubble? If so, ask the Lord what he would like to do with it.
- What do you see now that there is no wall?

_____

_____

_____

_____

_____

_____

_____

_____

_____

_____

PART FOUR

Thank the Lord! He's so good and faithful. He loves to lead us into freedom and it's vital that we recognize that we have an important part to play in staying free. Ask the Lord what guardrails he wants you to put into place so you don't begin to rebuild the wall.

_____

_____

_____

_____

_____

_____

_____

_____

_____

_____

If you were able to tear down an emotional or spiritual wall, that's amazing! If you saw a wall and were not able to tear it down because you didn't feel safe or ready, that's OK! You have permission to keep working on it, either through this kind of exercise or with the help of a therapist. The Lord is good to reveal it to you and you can trust that he is not disappointed or frustrated. His love is patient and kind, and all of his good work will come to fruition in your life. Pray with me:

> *Lord, thank you for your power and love. Thank you for tearing down walls and leading me into wholeness. I want to live free and stay free. I am asking you, Holy Spirit, to heighten my senses to the things that tie me down. I trust you and will rely on your goodness and wisdom.*

Chapter 9:

Emotional Healing

Joy verse

"Those who look to him for help will be radiant with joy; no shadow of shame will darken their faces."—Psalm 34:5 NLT

Warning: This story has a pretty gross analogy at the end. I promise it's worth it for the point. You've been warned.

My husband and I had been married almost two years when we attended a spiritual retreat with a group from our seminary. The spiritual director had spent a good amount of time teaching on the love of God and in order to activate us in our confidence, he had us do a simple yet profound exercise. We formed a large circle in the room and were instructed to, one at a time, turn to the person next to us and say, "John, God loves you." John would then turn to the next person, state their name and say the same thing. After it reached the end of the circle, we were to change the sentence to, "John, God loves me."

The first part was a cinch. It's easy to tell someone that God loves them! But for some reason the second part became much more vulnerable. As the second round reached me, I looked at my husband standing next to me and with great vulnerability and intimacy I said, "Kristopher" (I call him that when I am jokingly mad or when I am being sweet), "Kristopher, God loves me." To which he replied with a haughty laugh and smarmy tone, "Heck ya, I do." The oxygen was sucked out of the room. I froze. Everyone was looking at us, they all heard it. I was at the same time angry and disgusted, and humiliated for both myself and him. All I could muster up was "gross," with daggers in my eyes, of course. He quickly said, "Season, God loves me" and the ripple continued around the circle. The moment the exercise finished, the director said, "Now grab your blankets, chairs, and journals, go find a secluded spot and take two hours of silence and reflection with Jesus." All I wanted to do was yell at my husband, "How could you?! You're such a jerk!" But, not only were we at a monastery where we had to be quiet and mindful of those around us, we had been assigned silence!

Avoiding any eye contact with my husband I grabbed my stuff and headed off to be with Jesus (and my angry thoughts). Once I plopped down, I opened my journal and began to write, tears dripping onto the page. I told Jesus how humiliated I was, how my husband had ruined and stolen such a powerful moment for me with his pride and arrogance. To which the Lord replied, "I know, isn't it sad?" "What?! No! It's not sad, it's disgusting!" He continued, "It breaks my heart that he was so afraid to say it himself." What Jesus said, next changed the way I saw my husband and how I see everyone who hurts me. "That wasn't your husband talking, it was his wounds pussing."

I then saw a vision of my tough, strong husband as a little boy. He wasn't strong, he was tender and covered in scrapes, cuts, and bruises and some of his wounds were infected. My heart broke for that little boy, the one who was still inside of my husband. Jesus, saw that. He saw the raw infected wounds of shame, self-hatred, and rejection lashing out and getting all over me.

No longer was I mad; I was broken with compassion for my beloved husband. I saw him the way Jesus saw him. I spent the rest of the time praying for him and repenting for the ways I've been impatient or unkind to him. The Lord was so kind to show me this vision, and he lovingly began to show me *my* wounds and the effect their puss has had on others.

It's gruesome but it's accurate. Our wounds don't just have a deep impact on us, they have a huge effect on those around us. Even if we don't acknowledge them, we all have wounds from our past that have shaped our lives, our personalities, and the way we interact with others. When avoided, left unexamined, or blatantly ignored, those wounds often become infected and harm others.

At the risk of using another gross analogy, I am not a fan of water bottles. From my experience (with three kids and an athlete for a husband), most of the time they aren't actually filled with water. When you find them under the seat in your car, behind the couch, in a teenager's bedroom, or finally open the one that's been sitting in the sink for way too long, what greets you is more like a science experiment. And cleaning them is almost impossible! The openings are too small for your hand to fit and the curves and ridges make it so that no scrub brush can reach to ensure thorough cleaning. I have tossed many bottles for the fear of what's actually left growing even after my best efforts.

We are like those vessels, meant to be filled with the fresh, clean, living water of God's goodness. Filled to not only fuel ourselves, but to flow out to others. But like the mold and gunk left in the bottles, the wounds in our lives that aren't attended to, can taint and turn the fresh water that's poured in from Jesus to something that's quite contaminated and gross when poured out. I have seen wonderful and well-meaning Christians cause a lot of pain and strife unintentionally pouring out pride, greed, lust, fear, and division instead of goodness, love, and joy. By the grace of God, we are not required to be perfect to be used by the Lord. He uses us despite our shortcomings and sin. By intentionally pursuing healing and growth, we can help limit the cleanup. Our emotional healing is vital in becoming a Joy Bringer.

Name change

Jesus loved to heal emotional wounds because it restored identity. He brought the rejected into community (Matthew 9:10). He covered shame and humiliation with his presence and love (John 8:1-11). Jesus had compassion and healed the brokenhearted (John 11:21). Just like physical healings, Jesus had many tactics in healing emotional pain and restoring identities.

Some of my favorite moments in scripture are when God gives people new names. From Abram to Abraham, Sarai to Sarah, and Simon to Peter. God loves to change our identities, position, and mission by renaming us. My favorite name change is a subtle one, one that isn't included in the online search for "Who gets a name change in the Bible?"

We meet her in Luke 8:43-48 as she is clawing her way through the crowd desperate to touch just a piece of his robe. Jesus knew immediately, even though people surrounded him, that someone with great desperation and faith had touched him. Referred to as "woman"—more specifically, the "woman with the issue of blood"—she was identified by her suffering. She was known for her pain and shame. This woman didn't belong, just by being there she was out of bounds. But after twelve years of being unclean and feeling tired, she had reached the point where she didn't have any more cares to give. Jesus was her only hope. When he asked, "Who touched me?", she broke down in front of him, poured out her heart and explained that with one touch she had been instantly healed. That moment, Jesus renamed her. "Daughter," he said, "your faith has made you well." She is the only woman Jesus calls "daughter" in scripture.

The word "well" is more accurately translated as "whole." Jesus healed her of her physical ailment, but he also changed her identity from alone, broken, and ashamed, to loved, whole, and free.

Throughout our lives we become experts at avoiding, hiding, coping, and numbing our pain. The lengths we will go through to avoid pain is fascinating. At the same time, we will go to greater lengths to avoid healing. I love this quote from author Maxie Dunnam, "Most people prefer the hell of a predictable situation rather than risk the joy of an unpredictable one." Many of us have been with our wounds for so long they have become a part of our identities. Like the woman with the issue of blood who pushed past the fear of the unknown and reached out to experience God's goodness and healing power. I can tell you from my own experience with emotional healing and from the privilege I've had to journey alongside hundreds of others through it, the risk is so worth the reward!

Radiant with joy

"Those who look to him for help will be radiant with joy; no shadow of shame will darken their faces."—Psalm 34:5

I was raised in a conservative Christian home and have loved Jesus since I was very small. My mom was passionate about educating me about the "sin of premarital sex" and how "abortion was murder." And it worked...for a while. As a teen, I was legitimately terrified to have sex. I was convinced that not only would I be immediately struck down by lightning straight from the hand of God, but that my mother's sixth sense would inform her, and she would kill me. It would be a double murder, and I would go straight to hell.

Fast forward to age 25. I was in a committed relationship heading toward marriage and I found myself pregnant. I was using zero form of birth control but still totally shocked by this discovery. Duh, sex works! Naive and in my invincible 20's, I couldn't believe what was happening to me.

You would think that based on my love of Jesus, my conservative Christian upbringing, and the fact that I was in a marriage bound relationship, I would have just told my family and given my mother what she always wanted—a grandbaby. Nope. I was terrified.

Growing up in my home, there was a lot of unintentional projected shame and villanization toward not only premarital sex, but unwed mothers. I was convinced I would be disowned.

Pause. I must tell you that was not actually the truth. My mother and family would not have reacted this way, but in my fear and unwillingness to see my mother as a compassionate human being (which she was), it was easier for me to keep the truth hidden deep beneath fear.

I reached out to a close friend who I knew had multiple abortions. Next to my boyfriend, she was the only one I told. In fact, I took the pregnancy test at her house. According to her, the experience was easy, cheap, and not really a big deal. In the fog of fear and selfishness, it seemed like the best way to handle it because "the problem" just needed to go away. My boyfriend agreed. I rationalized it in a multitude of ways. My friend was right. It was quick, easy, virtually painless, and only $250 (which my boyfriend paid for). I was in and out within an hour and we were back at his place to binge watch movies for the day. No one knew, and I was going to keep it that way.

One year later I was lying in my bed, tears streaming down my face, and my brand-new husband trying to comfort me. But my mom had died in her room at the end of the hall a few hours earlier and I was gutted. So many visions and thoughts going through my head but the most prominent one, "Well, she knows now."

The torture of keeping my secret from her was gone. I found some solace in the idea that the grandbaby my mother so desperately wanted was waiting for her in heaven. Strange that I couldn't acknowledge I was pregnant with an actual baby, but I could imagine that her grandchild was in heaven. It was easier to hold onto the good rather than acknowledge the pain.

Eventually, all my rationale stopped working. My marriage didn't last long, I never had children of my own, and the pain of my secret was beginning to surface.

I understood that, technically, I was forgiven. I had repented countless times and had faith in the grace of God to cover my sins. However, I had not released the shame and pain that was associated with having had an abortion. It was just easier to pretend that it didn't exist, so I never told anyone, and I never used the A-word.

· Over the next few years, I embarked on a healing journey to address other pain in my life. I gained freedom from the pain of my divorce, the death of my mother, and I began to understand my worth and value as a daughter of the King and not in my profession. My life was changing dramatically for the better. I was in seminary, married an amazing man and became an insta-mom, and all the while, the Lord kept gently extending the invitation to actually "deal with the abortion."

I became a pastor and was heavily involved in a prayer and healing ministry. I saw the Lord do amazing things to free people from bondage and decided it was time for me to be free. I gathered some trusted friends to walk me through an emotional healing session. I had been a part of many of them and, for the most part, I knew what to expect. The person being prayed for asks the Holy Spirit to highlight a memory that the Lord would like to heal. It is never intended to cause more harm or re-traumatize, but only to reveal God's goodness and love in a painful moment. The results are powerful.

As we began, I was nervous. I had convinced myself that while I was forgiven, what I did was just about the worst thing one could do, surely there was no way that the Lord could show up during that.

With a deep breath, I asked the Holy Spirit to bring to mind a memory. A moment before, during or after my abortion, and reveal to me where Jesus was. I expected to see a picture of me sitting in the waiting room, or in the car on the way home. Nope. Immediately, I saw myself smack dab in the middle of the procedure, in the chair, the doctor doing his thing. And here's where it gets crazy: Jesus was there! He revealed that He was standing right next to me, holding my hand! But it doesn't stop there, He brought my mother with him. They were both standing next to me, holding my hand during the procedure.

Now you may be wondering, "What in the world is she talking about? How is that possible?" The truth is that God is outside of our timeline and it's totally possible for Him to take us back in our mind to see the spiritual reality of any situation. In my case, the physical reality was that my mother was alive when I had the abortion with no idea about what was happening. But God, in all his grace and mercy, brought her with Him to show me how loved I really am. In that moment, every chain shattered.

The two people who love me the most in all the universe, were loving me right where I was. They weren't cheering me on, or celebrating what was happening, but they were there with love and compassion. Not one twinge of shame, anger, or condemnation, just love. That's how good God is.

Everything changes when King Jesus shows up. Shame is eclipsed when the glory of God shines. There is no room for condemnation when the loving eyes and arms of Jesus are wrapped around you.

I am not proud of my decision, and I do not celebrate my choice. I do, however, celebrate the healing and love that is available for all people because of the total and complete forgiveness of Jesus Christ. I have no shame about having had an abortion because Jesus took it all away. Because of him I am radiant with joy.

Whether or not you have had an abortion, odds are there are wounds and dark places in your heart that you have hidden and protected from the eyes of the world. The Lord wants to heal those wounds and free you from their bondage. He did it for me, and he can do the same for you.

Our wounds are often attached to specific memories. Even if our pain developed over time, there are specific instances where we make associations. Like any wound, in order for it to heal, it needs to be cleaned out. As we have seen in our study of Jesus's ministry, things changed when he showed up. By inviting the Holy Spirit to highlight something that he wants to heal, you need to ask him to lead you to a specific memory. This is where the Lord in all his goodness and mercy shows up and off! You don't need to be afraid. This is only intended to bring healing. I have seen the Lord do mighty things. He can do whatever he wants so he may take you to a memory you remember or one you don't. He may take to you something before, during, or after a time of pain, or he may take you to a joyful place to reveal the truth in a different way. I have seen it all done with goodness, glory, and freedom.

When a memory or vision comes to mind, ask Jesus to reveal himself. While you may not have known he was even with you, he was! And he has something to say to you about the moment. He wants to show you where he was, what he thinks about it, and tell you the truth. His truth, presence, and deep love for you will change almost everything. Why almost? It won't change history. It cannot be undone, but it can change your view of it. His presence and love, his words of truth can radically alter the moment.

Jesus showed up.

Here are two short examples:

As a little girl I loved dance class. Performing in the recitals was my favorite, but I hated the getting ready part. There were always tears and arguments when my mom would put makeup on me and do my hair. I didn't realize that I had some real wounding around this and had believed some strong lies about my looks and value. As I asked the Lord to reveal to me a place he wanted to bring truth and healing, I was taken to an emotional moment as I was sitting on the bathroom counter begging my mom to not make me look like a raccoon (as I used to say) with all the blue eyeshadow. Asking Jesus to reveal himself, I immediately saw him standing behind my mom while she was doing my makeup. He was looking over her shoulder at me with such a funny face! He agreed with me, it looked silly. I asked him what he thought, and he told me that I was beautiful the way I was, without all that stuff on my face. He also told me that my mom thought the same thing and didn't realize what she was doing. Then the moment skipped ahead to the end of the night, Jesus was helping to wash off my face, he kissed my clean forehead and said, "You're my beautiful Season." Jesus invited me to forgive my mother. He also invited me to tell that little girl that she was beautiful. That wasn't easy!

The words we speak over ourselves are powerful. The Lord not only wants us to receive his love but to love ourselves. His presence and revelation didn't change what happened or erase the years of struggle with my looks and the way I saw myself. It did, however, change the way I now see myself and it removed the sting of the past. I will never forget his face, laughing at the foolishness of the raccoon eyeshadow, and his utter delight in me (and my mother), nor will I forget that kiss...I can still feel it.

My husband asked the Holy Spirit to take him to a memory. He saw himself (as a boy) as he a was finishing cleaning his dirt bike. He asked his dad to come look at it and his dad said, "It's still not as clean as your brother's." Deep pain of worthlessness, shame, and rejection filled his heart. He saw his little self sitting against the garage door, full of sadness. Jesus moved in behind him, took off his own crown (He was wearing a crown in this vision. Jesus can show up any way he likes!) and put it on my husband's head. It slipped down on his forehead because it was too big for him. It was in that moment when Jesus identified him as worthy! He was royalty and nothing could change that. My husband had a chance to ask the Lord how this moment made him feel and what truth he had to reveal to him. The words Jesus spoke shattered the worthlessness. It healed the bitterness and took away the anger toward his father.

JOY BRINGER CHALLENGE

Now it's your turn. You can do it! You may follow these steps and read these prayers and statements, or you are safe to simply be led by the Lord. I bless you with a beautiful, powerful, and healing encounter! Say this prayer:

Holy Spirit, I trust you. Would you take me to a moment you would like to heal? I give you permission to fully access my mind and my heart.

As you see a picture or recall a memory, allow yourself to be drawn into it. If nothing comes right away, give it some time and remember that the Lord is creative and often very surprising, so go with it and trust him.

Once you're aware of the moment (whether you remember it or not), take note of what's going on. What's happening? How are you feeling? This is where your experience is unique to you. I'm not with you so I can't help navigate, but you have the ultimate guide!

As you have a greater understanding of what's going on, invite Jesus to reveal himself. He may already have! But depending on your situation, here are a few things you may want to say:

- *Jesus, this is a hard and painful moment. I don't feel safe. There was great trauma and pain and I need to know, were you there? Where are you? What are you doing? Please reveal yourself.*
- *Jesus, I am not sure why you've shown me this moment, but I want to know more! Reveal yourself. Where are you and what do you want me to know?*
- *Thank you, Lord, for revealing yourself to me in this memory. Would you tell me how this moment made YOU feel?*

I pray you are experiencing powerful truth and healing because of the presence of Jesus. He never shows up with condemnation or accusation, but with compassion and love. You are loved, forgiven, and safe. Now may be a wonderful time to partner with Jesus in forgiveness. Depending on your situation, there may be an opportunity to forgive someone who has harmed you, or to forgive yourself for a choice that caused you or others harm. The next chapter has a great outline to walk you through forgiveness. (Spoiler alert: That's what's next!)

Now let's get even more clarity and truth! Ask the Lord these questions and write down what he says. Here are the questions:

- *Jesus, what lies have I believed because of the pain from this moment?*
- *Jesus, will you tell me the truth about this situation?*
- *Is there something you want me to tell myself?*
- *Is there anyone I need to forgive?*
- *Lord, how do you want me to remember this memory from now on?*

Write down the things you've seen and heard.

_____

_____

_____

_____

_____

_____

_____

_____

_____

_____

What you just experienced was real. The Lord is beyond our time frame and outside our limits. He can show up and do a mighty work anytime and anywhere, even in your mind. I bless you to let it all sink in and then go back for more! I do this all the time. It doesn't have to be a distant memory. If I have a troubling run-in with someone and I am hurting, I will ask the Lord to reveal where he was and what he has to say. Even in the joy-filled moments it's fun to ask the Lord to reveal himself and experience his joy too!

Go even deeper and have some fun with these:

- Ask Jesus to show you the spiritual reality in the room as you were being born. What was happening? How was heaven celebrating? Where was Jesus?
- Ask the Lord to show you the party that broke out in heaven when you said yes to Jesus (Luke 15:7).

King Jesus, thank you for your presence. Even when I didn't know you were there. I know that you are good and have never left me. Thank you for your protection and love. I declare that the truth you revealed to me today is real and the effects are permanent. Thank you for your desire to heal me. Thank you for the power of your Spirit to comfort and lead me into wholeness. I stand in awe of your love and radiate your glory.

Chapter: 10

Joy Bringer's Core Value– Forgiveness

Joy verse:
"Make allowance for each other's faults, and forgive anyone who offends you. Remember, the Lord forgave you, so you must forgive others."–Colossians 3:13 NLT

It's time for everyone's favorite subject, forgiveness. I know, I know, it's hard. But when it comes to our healing, it's vital. Like exercise, most of us agree that it's something we should do, but gosh it's difficult to not only start, but continue! Also, like exercise, when done it has incredible benefits. Forgiveness is the second Joy Bringer's Core Value (remember the first is Gratitude).

The enemy has an arsenal of weapons and one of his favorites is offense. He does everything he can to poke at the wounds. He wants us to be sore, protective, reactionary, and hold grudges. The more we stockpile bitterness, anger, and resentment the more we also reject the Lord's forgiveness. It's true! They are directly related. The truth is the enemy can't touch the victory of Jesus on the cross. He took all our sin and shame upon himself and paid the price. It's the best news ever! Thank you, Jesus. But what the enemy *can* do is try to convince us that we aren't really forgiven and get us to live like it, walking in shame and withholding forgiveness for others. But the gospel *is* good news, and we want to live like it.

When we acknowledge the magnitude of God's forgiveness in our lives it has a profound effect, one that begins with gratitude and results in the spread of the good news of great joy to the world at large. That may seem extreme, but forgiveness really is that big. These core values are meant to be everyday tools so we can live out the good news. We are to be filled with joy and bring it everywhere we go.

Before we dive into the tool of forgiveness, I want to give you an extra nugget that I find incredibly helpful. Offense is optional. You don't have to take it. You can choose to leave it right there. I have a friend who says, "I don't receive that" when something is said to her that could be taken as an insult or even a curse. We need to realize that first, most people aren't intending to offend. They are most likely blind to the impact of their words or actions due to their own woundedness or pain. Second, we have the power to see it for what it is (that's where wisdom and clear vision come in really handy) and choose not to take it. When insults, curses, or just plain rudeness is thrown our direction, we have a choice on what to do with it. We can get out of the way, bat it down, catch it and throw it back, or hold onto it and let it sink in.

I don't want to sound unreasonable and pretend that these arrows of offense don't hurt. They can and often do. But the clearer our vision becomes, the better we see not only the place where they came from but the reason they were thrown in our direction. And because of healing and the core value of forgiveness we have the power to say no to the offense. We can let it fly by, or if it hits, let it fall to the ground. Being on a journey of wholeness doesn't mean we don't get hurt, it means we have the tools to deal with the hurt when it comes. Forgiveness is the most comprehensive tool we have.

Shower prayers

I woke up in a cold sweat. Every muscle in my body was tense. I was screaming so loud in my dream that I wondered if I woke the neighbors. I thought I had buried all of that. I was trying to just move on and ignore how betrayed I felt. I wanted to forget that he lied to me, stole my money, and left without saying goodbye. Fifteen years of friendship was hard to ignore. Clearly, I needed to do something because that wasn't a dream I wanted to have again. So, I got in the shower. As I let the water wash the stress off my body, I began to talk to the Lord out loud.

"God, I'm in pain. I feel rejected by so many. My husband doesn't want me and now my close friends have betrayed me as well. I don't want to live like this. I know I need to forgive them to really move on. So, Lord, I declare that I forgive Zach (not his name). I really don't know if I mean it, but I am committed to say it 'til I get there."

Each day I stood in the shower, and I said, out loud, "I forgive him." Some days I would immediately walk it back, and other days I would feel confident enough to pray for blessings over his life. Eventually my shower prayers were filled with praying for his heart, his life, and his friendships. The crazy thing was I even released him from the debt. I didn't expect him to repay me or apologize. I had no contact with him and was truly at peace.

This was such a powerful exercise, so I decided to make a list. I took a legal pad and asked the Lord to bring to mind all the people I needed to forgive, and I began to write down the names. As I turned the page and still had more to write, I realized that this was long overdue. There were people on the list that really surprised me! People I wanted to make excuses for and release from their guilt, like my mother who was dead. I knew she and others didn't mean to hurt me. It was too painful to look under the layer of grief and hold her accountable for my pain. But the Lord informed me that it wasn't about them. I didn't need to worry about dishonoring or being disrespectful. I was safe to do the work.

Forgiveness isn't about the other person as much as it is about you. Ever heard the saying, unforgiveness is like drinking poison and expecting the other person to die? The fact is that your bitterness, anger, and resentment doesn't necessarily have much effect on the one it's directed toward. It does, however, have a significant effect on you and those around you. It can eat us alive! It can sour our other relationships. I knew someone who was so angry and bitter that they would brag about how much they hated their offender. They would proudly tell anyone who would listen, "If I ever see (so and so) on fire in the middle of the street I wouldn't even spit on them!" This was said with so much pride it was shocking and probably didn't have the desired effect on those around them. Instead of joining in on the hatred, I was moved by the immense pain I saw and frankly, I didn't want to be around them very often. The stench of hatred and bitterness permeated the room.

Contrary to popular belief, forgiveness isn't an effect of repentance. For forgiveness to happen there doesn't need to be an apology because it isn't about them, it's about you. Does someone's remorse help? Sure, but if our healing was determined by other people's willingness to admit and acknowledge our pain then we would be tied in knots waiting a long time. Back to my list.

As I reached the end, I heard the Lord say, "What about me?" I was a bit stunned and confused. "What do you mean, Lord? I can't forgive YOU; you've never done anything wrong!" I left his name off my list and went about my task of forgiving one at a time. It felt really good, and it was getting way easier!

About six months into the process (it was a long list!) I received two separate and unrelated messages through Facebook from women I went to middle and high school with. I didn't have a relationship with them in my adult life and one of the women I didn't remember at all. Both were beautiful notes of apology for being unkind and treating me poorly in school. I couldn't believe it! I didn't remember the encounters they mentioned, and I hadn't held any pain from them specifically, but what goodness and grace! The next week, I received a message from my friend Zach.

We met at a coffee shop. I went into this meeting with an arsenal of comebacks at the ready but they went unused. His apology was so sincere and comprehensive. He brought up and repented for things all throughout our (at the time) eighteen years of friendship. It was amazing. I was stunned. I shared with him the forgiveness journey I had been on and that I was able to release the bitterness, anger, and resentment and sincerely bless him. It was such an unexpected gift of God's abundant love.

Many years later, after I had become a forgiveness expert (well, maybe that's a stretch), the Lord brought it back up. "I want you to forgive me." Again, I wrestled. How can you forgive a perfect God? And how could I admit that I was angry or hurt by him? Wouldn't that make me a bad Christian? Once again, the Lord in his goodness led me to more truth.

Being disappointed, angry, or hurt by God isn't a sin. It's not about what God did to me or someone else, it's about how I have set my expectations on a throne. When my comfort, my desires, and my perspectives are challenged or not met there is emotional fallout. It's only natural to be sad or angry, disappointed, and bitter when our expectations aren't met. But God, in his kindness and love led me to see these wounds buried in my heart so I could be free from them.

When Jesus chose to not rush to the side of his dear friend Lazarus to save him from sickness and death, Mary and Martha were devastated. Jesus could have saved their brother but chose to stay where he was days longer. How hateful! How awful! How wrong they were. Jesus had a bigger plan. He was not only going to bring Lazarus back to life, he was foretelling his own resurrection. They were confused, deeply hurt, and yet grateful he was there. Jesus understood their disappointment and anger. He knew they didn't understand. Instead of defending himself or shaming them for their feelings, he met them with compassion. He listened to them and wept with them; he even felt their anger. Then he blew their minds with his goodness (John 11:1-44).

The hidden unforgiveness toward the Lord was eating away at my hope and joy. I was slowly becoming cynical and defeatist. Instead of agreeing with hope and victory, wondering how God would bring breakthrough and glory, I would worry and play worst case scenarios on repeat in my head. Unacknowledged disappointment and pain eventually led to hopelessness, depression, and anxiety. After seeing how it had manifested, I wanted it gone. My heart's desire was to trust the Lord completely and always agree with his goodness and glory. So, I began to be honest with God about what he already knew.

Forgiveness is a Joy Bringer's Core Value, it's also a command. Yes, a command from Jesus, not merely a suggestion (Luke 6:37). Forgiveness is the serious business of heaven because our forgiveness cost the Father everything. Jesus gave his life so that we could be forgiven. Let's read what Paul has to say about forgiveness in Ephesians 4:31-32. He said:

"Get rid of all bitterness, rage, anger, harsh words, and slander, as well as all types of evil behavior. Instead, be kind to each other, tenderhearted, forgiving one another, just as God through Christ has forgiven you."

Jesus understands how hard it can be. When we sit with the weight of what he did for us, we gain the strength to do it ourselves. It can feel impossible, you may even be thinking you'd rather suffer than forgive someone. But the good news is Jesus already suffered for you and your suffering is not necessary. He demonstrated that forgiveness puts to death the weight of sin and its effects, and new abundant and powerful life is restored.

I'm on this journey with you. There are days when I am practically levitating with hope and expectation, and others when hope is merely a flicker. These Joy Bringer Core Values are ones I use almost daily. They have helped me stay connected to the Lord's goodness and filled with joy. Making forgiveness a core value in your life will change the way you live and love.

JOY BRINGER CHALLENGE

I challenge you to make a list and get started today. Here is a forgiveness model that I have used that will help you as well as a comprehensive explanation and examples. I am with you in this!

I am so grateful for the teachers in my life. I value learning and at every opportunity I choose to sit at the feet of wisdom. This model is from my friend, Pastor Ann Hansen from Centerpoint Church in Murrieta, CA.

I forgive_____(name) for_____ (what was said / done)

Because it made me feel _____.

*Surrender those feelings to Jesus
I bless _____(name) with _____
(what they need)
I bless myself with _____. (what was taken from you)

STEP ONE

I forgive _____(name) for _____ (what was
said / done)

Remember what Jesus said in Matthew 18:21-22:

> *Then Peter came to him and asked, "Lord, how often should I forgive someone who sins against me? Seven times?"*
> *"No, not seven times," Jesus replied, "but seventy times seven!*

When we forgive it's important to state specifically what it is we've been hurt by. It is not limited. This is your healing journey and it's between you and the Lord. Nothing is off limits. Remember that we want to forgive not just someone's actions but also their words (or lack thereof). They can cause just as much pain and trauma in our lives (the "sticks and stones can break my bones, but words will never hurt me" saying is a total lie!). The important thing to remember here is to get it all out.

STEP TWO

Because it made me feel _____

Remember God's words of wisdom in Ephesians 4:26-27:

> *"Don't let the sun go down while you are still angry, for anger gives a foothold to the devil."*

This was a game changer for me! The hurtful actions and words are more obvious when it comes to forgiveness. I like to say that those things wind up on the shelf of anger, bitterness, and resentment. But it's the feelings that we carry around with us. Here's an example:

Your best friend Gary was house-sitting for you and forgot to blow out a candle when he went to bed. Tragically, the house caught fire and, while Gary made it out alive, all your belongings were destroyed. Gary is immensely sorry. Thankfully, the insurance company was able to rebuild your home. You can forgive Gary for burning your house down. He didn't do it on purpose. But what you are left with is fear, distrust, and trauma. Those are the things that you carry around on a daily basis and affect many areas of your life.

We must acknowledge the way someone's words or actions made us feel to really clean out the wound. Again, there is no limit to the list. The Holy Spirit will lead and highlight the way. Surrender those feelings to Jesus. Let's read about it in Matthew 11:28-30. It reads:

> *Then Jesus said, "Come to me, all of you who are weary and carry heavy burdens, and I will give you rest. Take my yoke upon you. Let me teach you, because I am humble and gentle at heart, and you will find rest for your souls. For my yoke is easy to bear, and the burden I give you is light."*

Now that you've listed the feelings, we get to surrender them to Jesus. He loves the great exchange, your heavy burden for his light one (Matthew 11:30). You can say something like this:

Thank you, Jesus, for your forgiveness and healing. Thank you that all of my pain matters to you. I recognize that I've been so burdened by these things, and I don't want to carry them or their effects around with me anymore. So, in the name of Jesus, I surrender the feelings of (state your list) to you, and I receive your peace and love in return. I am so grateful, and I love you.

STEP THREE

I bless _____ *(name) with* _____
(what they need)

"Bless those who curse you. Pray for those who hurt you."—Luke 6:28

Here it is! Another game changer. Seriously though, this one is where it's at. When Jesus forgives us, he doesn't do it with a cold shoulder. When we receive his forgiveness, we are brought into the family of God as sons and daughters. We become co-heirs with Christ, given a seat at the family table and an inheritance to boot. Now, I am not saying that we need to reconcile with our offenders or restore our relationship with them (oftentimes, that's not even possible). But we can pray and declare blessings on them and their lives. When you get to the point where you can bless the one who hurt you, you know you've done the work. (If the person has passed away then there is no need to include this step).

Jesus did it. He blessed those who cursed him, killed him, and betrayed him. He prayed for the souls of those who executed him. He shared a meal at the table and a kiss with Judas. Talk about taking the high road! According to scripture, the power of the blessing far outweighs the curse. I'll share much more later in this book but for the purpose of complete forgiveness, it helps to fill the hole that pain and bitterness bore, with power and godly action.

I was meeting with a woman who was fed up with her husband's abusive ways. It had become too much and she needed to leave. She was so angry. She hated him and was speaking curses over him. I told her that I deeply understood her anger but I couldn't encourage her to curse her husband, instead I told her to bless him. She was shocked and appalled. I continued. "I want you to bless your husband in your anger. Bless him to see you as his wife and the mother of his children. Bless him with conviction and a sensitivity to the Spirit. Bless him with a life changing encounter with Jesus and to experience his love. Bless him with healing and wholeness. Bless him to be aware of the pain he has caused. Bless him to be accountable for his actions." Blessing someone isn't about hoping they have a good day or win the lottery. We can bless them with what they need. We can pray for their hearts and minds to be touched and freed by the love of Jesus.

What helps in this process is to realize that we also have caused great pain in other people's lives. We've been marked by the kindness and goodness of the Lord, forgiven and blessed when we did nothing to deserve it. I am so grateful for the Lord's grace and mercy in my life, and I receive it from him, and I realize the importance of offering it to others.

STEP FOUR

I bless myself with _____ *(what was taken from you).*

Remember what scripture says in 1 Chronicles 4:10: "'Oh, that you would bless me and expand my territory! Please be with me in all that I do, and keep me from all trouble and pain!' And God granted him his request."

God loves to restore what was stolen and then some! Remember Job's story that's told in the Bible? Read the part of his story that is told in the book of Job, Chapter 42. As you read this scripture, you will see that the enemy loves to kill, steal, and destroy but God takes what was plundered and makes it full of life and abundance. We have the power to take back what was stolen by agreeing with heaven. Declaring truth over ourselves is partnering with the Lord and his gift of restoration and restitution.

There are many blessings in scripture. God blesses his people, fathers and mothers bless their children, and rulers bless their people. But there are times when those who should bless us just don't. There is a tiny mention of a man named Jabez in 1 Chronicles 4:9-10. There are a few things about this scripture that are important to note. First, it says he was named Jabez because it means that he caused his mother great pain in childbirth. What a wonderful daily reminder, "I'm a pain to my mom." Not really the most encouraging and empowering home life. Second, Jabez took it upon himself to pray for his own blessing. Clearly, he wasn't getting it from his family. Instead of sulking and waiting for someone to notice him, he simply went to the true source of blessing. God isn't offended when we pray for ourselves or declare blessing over our lives. It's what he wants! He wants us to be bold and audacious children, seeking goodness from our Father. He deeply desires us to be confident in his generosity and ask! Blessing ourselves with love, identity, wholeness, power, friendship, confidence and more helps our minds line up with the truth so we can walk in freedom and joy.

Section 3:

Filling

Joy verse:
"And the believers were filled with joy and with the Holy Spirit."
—Acts 13:52 NLT

Joy Principle:
Get fat on fruit!

Core value:
Flexibility

I don't like foods filled with what I describe as "goo." I say no "thank you" to jelly filled doughnuts, cream filled See's candy or pastries with simulated fruit inside. Those things freak me out. What if I bite into it and gross artificially flavored yuck fills my mouth?! But there is an exception, Cadbury Creme Eggs. You can keep your hollow chocolate bunnies, jellybeans, and Peeps. Cadbury Creme Eggs are hands down, my very favorite Easter treat. I love them so much that I must put a limit on how many I eat. Each year, I give myself one package (usually with five eggs in them). If I don't limit myself, I know I could have a 40-day feast!

My disdain for things with filling isn't unlike many Christians aversion to the Holy Spirit. It may sound strange to you if you've had a positive experience with the power and movement of the Spirit. But for others, the thought of being anything like "those people" running around, flailing, speaking in strange languages, being out of control and bizarre, is just enough to say, "No way! Not for me! You can keep your goo filled Christianity!" And I certainly don't blame you! My goal for this section is to introduce you to the person, purpose, and power of the Holy Spirit and help you move past the goo and onto the good stuff.

"I am a Christian." This is a statement that means far more than checking a box, but it seems to have lost much of its clarity and distinction. It means more than an eternity assignment or where one may spend a Sunday morning. The word "Christian" really means "little Christ." Being a Christian means being like Jesus Christ and doing the things he did. Jesus didn't call his followers Christians, he called them (and us), disciples. A disciple is one who learns and takes up the ways of another.

It seems strange that Jesus would only do three years of ministry on the earth. After a short 33 years on earth, he ascended into heaven. Oh, to have been there in those last moments! We don't know the full story, but we do know that he didn't intend his ministry to end with his ascension. He made it clear that we would carry on. He commissioned his disciples to not only do what he did but even greater things (John 14:12). Really?! That seems crazy when you think about it. How can anyone do greater things than Jesus? For some of us that's an exciting prospect, for others it may be a terrifying idea. Wherever you are on that scale, it's okay. Jesus never intended for us to do it on our own, he had a plan.

Jesus told the disciples in John 16:7, "It is best for you that I go away, because if I don't, the Advocate won't come. If I do go away, then I will send him to you." The plan all along was that Jesus would come to bring us new life and the Holy Spirit would come to empower us to live that life.

Remember that trust fall from chapter two? It's a risk! The more we know someone, the more confidence we have believing they will catch us. Odds are, you placed your trust in Jesus because you heard about him, read about him, and have talked to him in prayer. Most Christians would say they have a relationship with Jesus. That's great. But wait, there's more! The Trinity is a mysterious and complex subject: Three individual and unique persons—Father, Son, and Holy Spirit—but one God. Without shame or intentional wrongdoing, it's very common to connect with one or two members of the Trinity but leave out the other(s). Getting to know one member of the Trinity is getting to know God, but not knowing a member of the Trinity is missing out on the fullness of God.

If the thought of being totally surrendered to the Holy Spirit freaks you out, that's understandable. It's a risk to be sure. But like with any relationship, as you get to know the person of the Holy Spirit, your trust will grow. Remember what Jesus said in John 14:12: *"I tell you the truth, anyone who believes in me will do the same works I have done, and even greater works, because I am going to be with the Father."*

Jesus's exit from Earth was to give the Holy Spirit the opportunity to enter this world and fill every believer, therefore multiplying the power of Christ exponentially. Because of the Spirit we carry the power of the Almighty God with us. We do not worship (assign value) a myth or a historical relic. Our God is alive and with us! We are filled with the power and presence of the Holy Spirit to do the things Jesus has commissioned us to do.

Go! Tell! Heal! Bring joy!

Chapter 11:

Under the Influence

Joy verse

"And the believers were filled with joy and with the Holy Spirit."
—Acts 13:52 NLT

When I married into the Bowers family, I was quite overwhelmed with the size. As an only child I was not familiar with sibling culture and going from zero to three children overnight was quite the experience. It also didn't help that each daughter's name begins with the letter "A," and they all have middle names beginning with the letter "N." My husband and his whole family called each girl by not only their first names, but their middle names and a plethora of nicknames. You can imagine my confusion when everyone cycled through their many names with ease and clarity. I was totally lost!

One day, they were all talking about someone named Cass and I wasn't following. Finally, I asked, "Who's Cass?!" They laughed and told me that as a baby, our youngest daughter was bald with super white skin and bright blue eyes. Every time they would take a photo of her, her eyes would open wide, and she would look like she'd seen a ghost. They called her Casper, as in "the friendly ghost" (from a movie of the same title), which eventually shortened to Cass.

God has many nicknames in the Bible, in fact, there are over one thousand! While it's wonderful to have so many descriptive revelations about the personhood of God, it can be a bit confusing. God revealed his name to Moses in Exodus 34:6-7. His name is Yahweh. It is used over 6800 times, in almost every book of the Bible. Jesus has a name: Jesus of Nazareth. But the name for the third member of the Trinity isn't as clear.

The Holy Spirit (or Ghost) is a person but not human. Unseen, but often felt, heard, and revealed in other mysterious ways. It's perfectly normal to be unsure how to connect and relate. We often use the pronoun "he" but the Holy Spirit is not a man or a woman or an it. The third member of the Trinity is God, not an afterthought or an optional less important supporting character. Unfortunately, because of our language limitations and lack of understanding, we relegate Holy Spirit to a thing, one that is often left out of the equation. I think one of the best ways to get to know Holy Spirit is to look at a few of the other Biblical names and titles.

Spirit of God

Our first introduction to the Holy Spirit takes place immediately in Genesis 1:2," And the Spirit of God was hovering over the surface of the waters." From the beginning, the Trinity (the triune God), were at work together. I love that from the first words of the Bible, God reveals himself as a limitlessly creative God: "In the beginning God created the heavens and the earth" (Genesis 1:1). We are made in the image of God and each member has a unique but not limited expression of creativity. I like to think of Father

God as the great designer, Jesus as the Word of God who is the ultimate storyteller, and the Holy Spirit as inspiration and ability.

We see an example of the inspiration and ability from the Holy Spirit in the building of the tabernacle in Exodus. This is the first instance of someone being filled with the power of the Spirit. "The Lord has filled Bezalel with the Spirit of God, giving him great wisdom, ability, and expertise in all kinds of crafts" (Exodus 35:31). When we get to know the Holy Spirit, we can expect uniquely creative revelations of love and power.

Paraclete

One of the Greek names used for Holy Spirit is *paraclete*. Jesus uses this name to tell the disciples that after him will be one who comes and will never leave them. The word is defined as a comforter, counselor, advocate, and helper. That's a part of who Holy Spirit is; one who offers us security knowing that God is indeed with us in our trials and sorrow. One who intercedes on our behalf to the Father and who helps by empowering us with the power of Christ to do the things Jesus commissioned.

Spirit of Truth

Truth is truth, when you know it you know. Jesus also calls the Holy Spirit, "the Spirit of Truth." Let's read about it in John 16:13-15:

> *"When the Spirit of truth comes, he will guide you into all truth. He will not speak on his own but will tell you what he has heard. He will tell you about the future. He will bring me glory by telling you whatever he receives from me. All that belongs to the Father is mine; this is why I said, 'The Spirit will tell you whatever he receives from me.'"*

This is another reminder that the Father, Son, and Holy Spirit are united. Jesus says of himself that he is "the way, the truth, and the life" (John 14:6). Therefore, so is the Spirit of Truth. We can be sure that when we get to know the Holy Spirit, he will lead us into a deeper knowing of Jesus and the Father.

There are many mysteries surrounding God, I mean, we are talking about a *spirit*! Mysteries are not a bad thing. We are meant to be in awe and wonder of our infinite and glorious Creator. While there is no limit to what we can learn about the Lord, God is not a God of confusion. Through the Holy Spirit we receive revelation and truth leading us deeper into the heavenly mysteries of God and revealing to us greater wisdom and understanding for this world.

Convicter of Sin

Convicter of sin, how's that for a name? Maybe this is why there is a great avoidance of the Holy Spirit. Jesus says in John 16:7-11:

> "*If I do go away, then I will send him to you. And when he comes, he will convict the world of its sin, and of God's righteousness, and of the coming judgment. The world's sin is that it refuses to believe in me. Righteousness is available because I go to the Father, and you will see me no more. Judgment will come because the ruler of this world has already been judged.*"

I want you to catch something subtle here. Jesus says that the world's sin is unbelief. The Holy Spirit longs to lead us to a relationship with Jesus. Conviction is not condemnation or shame. Conviction is not accusation or humiliation. Conviction is the revelation of the beauty and holiness of God in contrast to the darkness of our sin. The Holy Spirit shines a light into the darkness so that we can be made aware of our need for Jesus. Scripture tells us that it's the kindness of the Lord that leads us to repentance. Jesus took the punishment of our sins so we could live in freedom and intimacy with the Lord. The Holy Spirit leads us to turn from the destructive and harmful sin in our lives and toward the goodness, love, wholeness, and freedom found in Jesus. We can be sure that his ways are always loving, never shameful or condemning. The Holy Spirit's desire is to make us more like Jesus.

Jesus lived his life as a model of the Kingdom of heaven on earth. He told us to pray for that to be manifested on earth as it is in heaven. He told us to be like him, doing the things he did and loving the way he loved. He did all of it without sin. But he didn't expect us to do it on our own, he gave us the power to do that through the gift of the presence of Holy Spirit.

The nicknames

One of the nicknames for our youngest daughter is "bug." Of course through the years that has morphed into, "buggy" or "bugalicious." We choose all kinds of strange names to refer to those we love, don't we? Fire, water, wind/breath, and a dove are names and symbols that bring even more clarity to the character and nature of the Holy Spirit.

Fire

I love a good bonfire. I was in my twenties when I realized that the word wasn't "bond-fire." When someone corrected me, I was shocked. I just thought it referred to what happened when people gathered around a fire—bonding! Fire warms, draws people close, and illuminates. So does Holy Spirit.

Fire also purifies. The big word is "sanctification." It means the process of the Holy Spirit making us holy, more like Jesus (1 Corinthians 6:11). In the Old Testament, the fire on the altar was a constant symbol of the presence and holiness of God. Now, we have become the temple of the living God and the indwelling of Holy Spirit is the fire that burns on the altar of our hearts (2 Corinthians 6:16).

The Holy Spirit helps us burn with passion for the Lord (Luke 24:32). When Jesus says we are the light of the world, he wasn't talking about an electric light bulb! We are walking, talking sources of light that lead the way to *the* light (Jesus Christ).

Water

Once you reach the point of thirst you are already dehydrated, that's why drinking water consistently is important. Water symbolizes life because we cannot live without it. Jesus said to the woman at the well in John 4:1-42 that he had a kind of water that would quench her thirst forever. The water he was referring to was the presence of the Holy Spirit (John 7:37-39). With the ever-present living God with us at all times we are never lacking. We have an unlimited supply of power, love, revelation, and refreshment.

Ezekiel 47:1-12 describes the river of life that flows from the throne of God. There will be swarms of living things wherever the water of this river flows. It brings constant nourishment and refreshment causing life to flourish in abundance. This is the power of the Holy Spirit. It is constantly flowing and moving, bringing power from the throne of God to us and through us to others.

Breath/Wind

It feels odd to refer to the third member of the Trinity as a spirit or ghost. Those things are spooky and strange. The Hebrew word used for The Holy Spirit is *ruach*, meaning, "air in motion." It's the same word used for breath and life. The same applies to the Greek word for Holy Spirit, *pneuma*, meaning "a current of air, breeze, or breath." The Holy Spirit's name is not referring to a spooky invisible being, it's referencing the life source of God filling us, being closer to us than our breath.

The first cry of a newborn is a beautiful thing. It indicates that there is breath, and breath means life. Genesis 2:7 says, "Then the Lord God formed the man from the dust of the ground. He breathed the breath of life into the man's nostrils, and the man became a living person." As God breathed life into Adam, Jesus breathed onto his disciples. Let's read about this story in John 20:20-22. Scripture says:

> *As he spoke, he showed them the wounds in his hands and his side. They were filled with joy when they saw the Lord! Again he said, "Peace be with you. As the Father has sent me, so I am sending you." Then he breathed on them and said, "Receive the Holy Spirit."*

The work of the breath of God starts from the beginning, from our first breath, and continues throughout our whole lives. It sustains and empowers. I think the words of Paul in Acts 17:25 say it best, "He himself gives life and breath to everything, and he satisfies every need." That's the Holy Spirit!

While you can't see wind, you can see and feel the effects of it. It can blow with a mighty gust or a gentle breeze. It can rustle the leaves of a tree or blow the roof off a house. Wind is a symbol of power and freedom. While we have learned to harness the wind as a resource and even produce it on our own, the natural resource of wind cannot be controlled or tamed. John 3:8 (NKJV) says, "The wind blows where it wishes, and you can hear the sound of it, but cannot tell where it comes from and where it goes. So is everyone who is born of the Spirit." As we continue to get to know the Holy Spirit and learn to trust and surrender to his leading, we will come to realize that being filled and powered by the wind of God means that we are to move with freedom and power.

JOYFUL DISCOVERY

I taught voice lessons for more than a decade. It was vital that my students understood the importance and power of their breath. Without air there is no sound. That's science. Vibrations of sound travel on airwaves. It's been proven that while they diminish in strength, sound waves never stop reverberating. This means that the words, "Let there be light (Genesis 1:3)." "It is finished (John 19:30)." "Talitha, cumi (Translation in Mark 5:41: "Little girl, I say to you, arise!") and "I am who I am (Exodus 3:14)" are still reverberating through our atmosphere. Close your eyes, hear those words, and let them touch your soul.

Dove

A logo or icon is intended to trigger immediate recall. You see the swish you think of Nike. You see the apple you think of Macintosh. If you see a cross or fish on a bumper sticker or necklace you know they represent Jesus. The same applies to a dove. It's a symbol for the Holy Spirit.

There are two major events in Scripture involving doves. The first is found in the story of Noah. After the rain had stopped, Noah sent out a dove to investigate. When it came back with an olive branch, they knew the waters had subsided from the earth. The dove was the first to find a home and new life on earth and became a symbol of God's peace after judgement.

In the New Testament, all four gospel accounts include the moment of Jesus's baptism where the Spirit of God descended on Jesus in the form of a dove. Once again, the dove shows up representing peace after judgement. Jesus's baptism foreshadows his death as the atonement for our sin, along with the peace, freedom, and power of new life. Let's read what scripture says about Christ's baptism in Matthew 3:16-17:

> *"After his baptism, as Jesus came up out of the water, the heavens were opened and he saw the Spirit of God descending like a dove and settling on him. And a voice from heaven said, "This is my dearly loved Son, who brings me great joy."*

I love this moment so much. Jesus in the water, the Holy Spirit affirming Jesus as the Messiah, and the voice of the Father declaring his delight.

There is a Swedish saying that translates, "A beloved child has many names." Whether you call him Spirit of God, Spirit of Truth, Breath, Wind, Fire, Holy Ghost or Holy Spirit, he is a loyal, constant, nourishing, powerful and loving guide. Doesn't that sound like someone you can trust? There are endless ways we are cared for and loved by the Holy Spirit. Call him what you will but getting to know our constant companion leads us to trust him even more.

Under the influence

I hate coffee. In my entire life I've never had a cup. Now don't get me wrong, I am not being good or self-controlled, I just don't like the taste. I have learned not to fall for peer-pressure anymore, "Try it! I *swear* it doesn't taste like coffee." Lies! It always does. However, I do still drink a dark, bitter substance that leaves me beautifully caffeinated. Black tea. English Breakfast is my favorite. But honestly, it's really just a vehicle for yummy creamers. I love a good, sweet, creamy hot tea. I mean, I *love* it! I can't wait to hop out of bed to indulge. Often because of my natural morning "perk" my husband will question my desire for the caffeinated boost, "Do you really *need* it this morning, babe?" To which I exclaim with ferocity in my eyes and a smile on my face, "*Yes!*"

I have been known to blame my passion and energy on being under the influence of both caffeine and the Holy Spirit. But to be fair to the Spirit, I stop my caffeine consumption before 2:00 p.m. or I will be up all night. Jesus knew the power of the Spirit and was excited for his disciples to experience it. "And now I will send the Holy Spirit, just as my Father promised. But stay here in the city until the Holy Spirit comes and fills you with power from heaven" (Luke 24:49). He realized they wouldn't totally understand but he knew what was coming. He couldn't wait for them to be acquainted with the Holy Spirit. I can imagine their confusion, "OK Jesus, sounds good. You died; you came back. That was great. Now you say you're leaving again, and we're supposed to just wait here for some *spirit*? Right." Fortunately, by that point they had enough experience walking with him to realize that what he said would come to fruition, no matter how strange it sounded. And boy, did it!

The day of Pentecost changed everything for the disciples. As they were gathered together in prayer and worship, flaming tongues of fire appeared above people's heads, sounds of rushing wind and languages—both known and unknown—were spoken so the people in the streets could hear. It was wild. They were "filled" with so much of the Holy Spirit that they were accused of being publicly intoxicated at ten in the morning. They weren't drunk with alcohol, but they were under the influence of the power of the Holy Spirit. That's what the word "filled" implies—being totally surrendered. Paul says in Ephesians 5:18-20 (NIV):

"Do not get drunk on wine, which leads to debauchery. Instead, be filled with the Spirit, speaking to one another with psalms, hymns, and songs from the Spirit. Sing and make music from your heart to the Lord, always giving thanks to God the Father for everything, in the name of our Lord Jesus Christ."

I love the implication here that being surrendered to the Holy Spirit and filled with the fullness of God, leads us to boldness, joy, and gratitude.

When we accept Jesus as our Lord and Savior, we are given the gift of the Holy Spirit (2 Corinthians 1:22) and he makes us his home. We often use the word "filled" to describe this indwelling. But there has been great debate about the timing or way to receive the baptism of the Holy Spirit. Isn't it just like the enemy to cause division and confusion to keep people from experiencing the goodness of God? I can't solve the centuries of debate regarding the power of the Holy Spirit. But I do know this to be true: God doesn't just give us a piece of himself. The Holy Spirit doesn't just live in us part-time or only stop by on the weekends.

Jesus tells us to ask, seek, and knock and the door will be opened (Matthew 7:7-8). The Lord wants us to know and experience all his goodness and great joy. As you've gotten to know the person of the Holy Spirit, it's my prayer that you want to know even more, to experience his presence and the power. "And the believers were filled with joy and with the Holy Spirit" (Acts 13:52).

JOY BRINGER CHALLENGE

Are you ready to surrender to the Holy Spirit? We have more to learn, but before we keep going, I challenge you to do a little private investigation. Have you made up your mind about the Holy Spirit? Are there things you've heard, seen, or experienced that have caused you to have reservations or even built a wall when it comes to the person, presence, or power of the Spirit? I invite you to ask yourself these questions then invite the Lord to reveal his insight and truth. The questions are:

- Do I have any aversion to Holy Spirit? If yes, where did it come from?
- Is there someone I need to forgive?
- Have I made any vows or agreements regarding the person, presence, or power of Holy Spirit? (Examples: the work of the Spirit stopped a long time ago, the Holy Spirit isn't God, I don't need to have strange experiences to know God, etc.)
- Am I afraid of the unknown?
- Am I afraid of what people would think of me?
- What is getting in the way of me experiencing more of the presence of God?

If you are ready to take a step forward into the mystery and wonder of the Spirit of God, tell the Lord! I cannot promise a specific outcome, but I can promise you that God hears and responds to your prayers.

Chapter 12:

Get Fat on Fruit

Joy verse

"But the Holy Spirit produces this kind of fruit in our lives:
love, joy, peace, patience, kindness, goodness, faithfulness,
gentleness, and self-control. There is no law against these
things!"–Galatians 5:22-23 NLT

My sister-in-law owns a plant nursery in Tennessee called Dirty
Girls Nursery (named by yours truly). I love being there. The
smell of the dirt, the warm greenhouses, the color and beauty of
the plants, it's all divine. When I can, I like to help fill pots with
soil, plant seeds, and occasionally they let me water the plants.
Every step in the growing process is important. Of course plants
grow on their own but it's the cultivation and care of the gardener
that helps to produce a good and productive harvest.

If the Holy Spirit had a profession, I believe it would be as a
gardener or farmer. A large part of the work of the Holy Spirit in
our lives is to help us cultivate and produce spiritual fruit. As we
grow in our desire to live loved by God and surrendered to his

leading, we need to be acquainted with the work and gifts of the Holy Spirit. It helps to know what we're signing up for!

All you can eat

Dream with me. You see it from across the room, the most beautiful perfectly crafted dessert tray straight from your fantasy vault of desserts. If only you could indulge! You are tempted but the sight alone makes your waistband tighter. You think, "Maybe just a bite? It's better than nothing." As the server brings the tray of temptation over to your table you are told, "There are virtually no calories in this delicious treat, and if you eat all of it you will be helping to end world hunger." The clouds part and you are in a vortex of heavenly glory. Permission to indulge! Two of each, please!

Oh, if only! Who doesn't want all you can eat of something delicious without the consequences?! In Galatians, Paul is writing to people who would have been very familiar with Hebraic law. They understood what they could and couldn't do, how much or how little of something they could have, as well as when and where they were to do just about everything. It's important to understand this context when we read the famous list of the fruit of the Spirit, so we catch the full meaning of what he's saying.

> *"But the Holy Spirit produces this kind of fruit in our lives: love, joy, peace, patience, kindness, goodness, faithfulness, gentleness, and self-control. **There is no law against these things!**"*—Galatians 5:22-23 (emphasis added)

Those last seven words are my favorite. Paul is letting his readers know that there really is a way you can tell if a person is a Christ follower. Like a tree, it will produce a certain kind of fruit—proof if you will. But he's also saying there is no law (or limit) to the amount of fruit of the Spirit we can have. That is total permission to stuff ourselves and get fat on fruit! In fact, that's exactly what the Lord wants for us. To be so full of fruit we are dripping with abundance. But there is a catch. It's up to us to cultivate.

Just like following Jesus takes intentional effort to put one foot in front of the other, so does the cultivation of the fruit of the Spirit in our lives. The mere presence of the Holy Spirit within us won't do the trick. If that were the case, most of us wouldn't have a least favorite fruit (come on, you know it's patience). If just the presence of the Holy Spirit caused us to produce abundant fruit, then we'd live in perfect harmony with everyone. It's the cultivating part that takes work. Jesus spends quite a bit of time on this subject in John 15:1-8 (NIV). He says:

> "I am the true vine, and my Father is the gardener. He cuts off every branch in me that bears no fruit, while every branch that does bear fruit he prunes so that it will be even more fruitful. You are already clean because of the word I have spoken to you. Remain in me, as I also remain in you. No branch can bear fruit by itself; it must remain in the vine. Neither can you bear fruit unless you remain in me.
>
> "I am the vine; you are the branches. If you remain in me and I in you, you will bear much fruit; apart from me you can do nothing. If you do not remain in me, you are like a branch that is thrown away and withers; such branches are picked up, thrown into the fire and burned. If you remain in me and my words remain in you, ask whatever you wish, and it will be done for you. This is to my Father's glory, that you bear much fruit, showing yourselves to be my disciples."

The Holy Spirit is the Spirit of God living within us. When we stay surrendered to the leading and cultivation of the Spirit, we will produce good fruit. Sounds easy enough, right? Well, if it was, we'd all be abundant fruit producers. There are quite a few challenges in the growing process.

Did you ever have growing pains as a child? I did, and they were rough! In order to grow we must endure the stretching and sometimes it hurts. It's that productive pain I wrote about in the first section. It's pain that is meant to help not harm. But because we are often so afraid of pain, we will go to great lengths to avoid it. Processes take time.

The word pruning doesn't sound so bad but what's challenging is what it means—cutting. Ouch! When I look at a beautiful fruit tree or rose bush with an abundance of beauty on it, I don't think, "I know what I should do, I should cut off those branches!" It doesn't make sense to us. But ask a gardener and they will get right in there and chop away! My sister-in-law said to me, "When you prune, you encourage even more growth. Cutting off what is not only dead or weak, but also only somewhat productive, will lead to a healthier and abundantly productive plant." It's exactly what Jesus says, when we go through a pruning process we end up with abundance.

Even when I know that pruning is good for the plant, it's sometimes still hard. I will look at a plant and think, "It looks great! I don't want to cut it back or lose what is already pretty good." We think this about ourselves too. "I'm a good person!" "I'm fine, I'm not hurting anyone." "I've grown so much already; you should have seen me a decade ago!" But again, pruning isn't just for dead branches or our sinful ways. This is why it was possible for Jesus to be pruned. He didn't have any bad branches, but he did grow and mature (Luke 2:52) and in order for that to happen, he had to be pruned. This is more proof that pruning isn't bad and only done to produce abundance.

The Lord isn't withholding his goodness from us. It's our own wounding and the lies of the enemy that keep us from desiring more. Fear keeps us from going deeper, stronger, taller, and producing even more fruit.

JOY BRINGER CHALLENGE

I want to be a bearer of abundant fruit. I want to be surrendered to the process of the good and loving gardener tending my life. In order to do that it's important to ask the question, "What would mature fruit look like in my life?"

Here is a challenge: Below, I have provided a brief description with scriptural references to explain further the meaning and examples of each fruit. **I challenge you to ask the Holy Spirit to reveal to you what a mature version of that fruit would look like in your life and write it down.**

Love: It's pretty clear that we often get this one wrong. Love isn't about our feelings, or our own satisfaction, it's about the other. Love is a verb—an action word. Unconditional love requires nothing from the recipient. Love takes courage, boldness, and vulnerability. Love for God and others is a result of receiving God's perfect love and letting it change us.

"Dear children, let's not merely say that we love each other; let us show the truth by our actions."—1 John 3:18 NIV

Also read:
- 1 Corinthians 13:4-8
- Philippians 2:3
- John 15:13
- 1 John 4:8

_____

_____

_____

_____

_____

_____

_____

_____

Joy: A buoyant sense of well-being because of the person and work of Jesus Christ, cultivated by the power and presence of the Holy Spirit, and because of the love of the Father. It is not circumstantial but a direct result of the presence and power of God. Joy is often expressed as happiness or upbeat energy. But joy is also experienced through calm, peaceful and quiet confidence.

"Consider it pure joy, my brothers and sisters, whenever you face trials of many kinds because you know that the testing of your faith produces perseverance."—James 1:2-3 NIV

Also read:

- Nehemiah 8:10
- 1 Chronicles 16:27

_____

_____

_____

_____

_____

_____

_____

_____

Peace: Peace is not dependent on our circumstances. It's a state of being confident in the presence and power of Jesus. It is also something we are called to actively pursue and foster in our lives and in all circumstances. Just as we are called to be Joy Bringers, we are also called to walk in the shoes of the gospel of peace, bringing it wherever we go.

"I have told you these things, so that in me you may have peace. In this world you will have trouble. But take heart! I have overcome the world."—John 16:33 NIV

Also read:

*   Colossians 3:15
*   Romans 8:6

_____

_____

_____

_____

_____

_____

_____

_____

_____

_____

Patience: Ah, the one fruit most people don't enjoy. But this fruit is the one of the most nutritious. It can also be called forbearance, long-suffering, perseverance, and endurance. The literal translation of the word is "long temper." The ability to wait with grace and hope in the goodness and faithfulness of God. Being patient doesn't imply weakness, on the contrary, it's powerful! Patience demonstrates confidence, compassion, love, and clear vision. It does not imply lack, it invites us to be satisfied in the Lord.

"I say to myself, "The Lord is my portion; therefore, I will wait for him." The Lord is good to those whose hope is in him, to the one who seeks him; it is good to wait quietly for the salvation of the Lord."—Lamentations 3:24-26 NIV

Also read:

- Hebrews 6:15
- James 5:7-8
- Psalm 5:3

_____

_____

_____

_____

_____

_____

_____

_____

_____

Kindness: It's a risk! Like love, kindness is an action word. The Lord demonstrates his tender loving kindness to us by giving us freedom, allowing us to live here and providing for us, even when we don't cherish or honor the gift. True kindness is unconditional, not expecting anything in return. Kindness isn't weak! Even if the "survival of the fittest," "dog eat dog," "looking out for number one" mentality gets associated with strength and power, those things are easy and not lasting. Kindness takes humility and love which are much more challenging and impactful.

"And be kind to one another, tenderhearted, forgiving one another, even as God in Christ forgave you." —Ephesians 4:32 NKJV

Also read:

• Philippians 2:3-4

_____

_____

_____

_____

_____

_____

_____

_____

_____

_____

Goodness: Jesus said, "Why do you call me good? No one is good—except God alone" (Mark 10:18). So what are we doing here? Goodness is similar to kindness but rooted deeper in the nature of God. Goodness is virtue and holiness in action. It goes beyond niceness and embraces and embodies truth in love. The only way to look more like our good Father in heaven is through a deeper surrender to the Holy Spirit. It is the Lord who cleanses us from sin and makes us righteous. Our goodness brings God glory.

"Don't just pretend to love others. Really love them. Hate what is wrong. Hold tightly to what is good."—Romans 12:9

Also read:

• James 1:17

_____

_____

_____

_____

_____

_____

_____

_____

_____

_____

_____

Faithfulness: If faith the size of a mustard seed can move a mountain, imagine what can be accomplished as your faith is cultivated with the Holy Spirit! God wants your faith to grow so you can live boldly and with confidence. God is trustworthy, faithful, and good. The more we come to really believe that the more we step out in faith. My best friend says it like this, "Belief is seeing the stop lights at the intersection and believing they are programmed correctly and will do their job. Faith is driving through the intersection." The Holy Spirit testifies to the faithfulness of God.

"Now faith is confidence in what we hope for and assurance about what we do not see."—Hebrews 11:1 NIV

Also read:

- 2 Corinthians 5:7
- Luke 17:19

_____

_____

_____

_____

_____

_____

_____

_____

_____

_____

_____

Gentleness: When something is of great value, we are sure to handle it with care. Imagine an archaeologist jumping on a shovel to uncover priceless artifacts. Gentleness is not weak or passive, it is honoring and loving. The same Jesus who stormed the temple with a whip was gentle with the sick, ashamed, hurting, and lost. Being gentle takes lenses of love to see others the way our loving God sees them. The Holy Spirit helps us temper our prideful and harsh reactions so others will know the grace of the Lord.

"Let your gentleness be evident to all. The Lord is near."—Philippians 4:5 NIV

Also read:

- Luke 9:56
- Matthew 11:29
- Isaiah 40:11

_____

_____

_____

_____

_____

_____

_____

_____

_____

_____

Self-Control: Why did Jesus never sin? While he was tempted, he knew the pure goodness of the kingdom of God! The seemingly instant gratification on earth paled in comparison to the pure satisfaction and wholeness he knew in purity and righteousness. The Holy Spirit isn't with us to keep us from the fun stuff, just the opposite! He wants to reveal to us the pure goodness and real satisfaction found in the love of God. Self-control is choosing God's goodness instead of the artificial stuff that leaves us unhealthy, unsatisfied, broken and ashamed.

"For God has not given us a spirit of fear and timidity, but of power, love, and self-discipline."—2 Timothy 1:7

Also read:

- Galatians 5:19-23
- 1 John 2:15-17
- Genesis 4:6-7

_____

_____

_____

_____

_____

_____

_____

_____

_____

JOY BRINGER CHALLENGE

Ask the Lord these questions and write down what you see and hear. These are the questions:

- Lord, will you show me a picture of what my fruit tree looks like to you?
- What fruit of mine is ripe and sweet?
- What fruit is small and underdeveloped?
- What would you like to prune in me so I can produce more fruit?

_____

_____

_____

_____

_____

_____

_____

_____

_____

_____

Chapter 13:

Superpower

Joy verse

"But you will receive power when the Holy Spirit comes upon you. And you will be my witnesses, telling people about me everywhere—in Jerusalem, throughout Judea, in Samaria, and to the ends of the earth."—Acts 1:8 NLT

There is a big disagreement in my house on whether or not cars or trucks should be loud. My husband likes his truck to growl. However, I do not enjoy the entire neighborhood knowing our comings and goings. That's not to say I don't enjoy the power and get up of a strong engine, I just don't prefer the roar. Everyone is different when it comes to our power preferences. The same goes for how we want to operate in the power of the Holy Spirit. No surprise here, the Lord already knows this about us and has tailor made gifts for each of his children enabling us to operate in the power of God.

Getting to know the person and purpose of the Holy Spirit isn't complete without knowing and receiving his power. It's like having a supercar in your driveway, beautifully made with all the latest bells and whistles. You know it looks good, you've even sat in it and it feels good. But you don't know anything until you've put the pedal to the metal and seen what she can do!

Jesus is described as the Lion and the Lamb. These are two different sides that have very specific purposes. There is a similar dichotomy with the Holy Spirit. He is comforting, nurturing, and helpful. But he is also powerful, wild, and supernatural. The Holy Spirit comes with power and wants us to let that power loose in the name of love for the glory of God! The gifts of the Spirit are not just for looks or show. The Holy Spirit is invisible, but we can see, hear, and feel his presence through the manifestations of his gifts. God uses these gifts to not only strengthen our faith but to reveal himself to us and others. That's what Jesus intended when he told the disciples, "You will receive power when the Holy Spirit comes upon you. And you will be my witnesses, telling people about me everywhere—in Jerusalem, throughout Judea, in Samaria, and to the ends of the earth" (Acts 1:8). The Lord wants us to have a full experience of his power and glory, not just head knowledge. He wants our encounter with him to be a part of what fuels the spread of the good news to the ends of the earth. God wants to use you as a conduit for others to experience his goodness as well. I like to think of the gifts as various expressions of the personality of God.

I remember going to work with my mother when I was a child and being fascinated. She was the same person, but I saw different sides of her. She was using a different skill set at her job and I loved watching her at work. There are a few lists of the gifts of the Spirit in scripture. Because each mention has some overlap and also variance, we can know that this isn't an exhaustive and comprehensive list. These gifts are diverse and a fitting example of the creative expressions of God's love for his children. The gifts are powerful tools used to build up the body of Christ. They are supernatural, meaning they come from the power of God, not from our own abilities (although the more we trust in God's power, the more confident we become to use the gifts).

I want to briefly introduce you to the gifts listed in Romans 12:8, 1 Corinthians 12:4-11 and 1 Corinthians 12:28. As you read, be aware of any feelings you have toward them. Let's explore these gifts:

Word of knowledge: A revelation or knowledge about something that you would have no ability or means of knowing.

Word of wisdom: Often partnered with a word of knowledge, this gift provides direction and clarity regarding a word of knowledge or particular situation. While everyday practical wisdom is available to us through prayer and Scripture, this gift is a supernatural manifestation of the Holy Spirit.

Prophecy: A word from the Lord given to someone to build them up and reveal God's love for them. It often includes a foretelling of the future.

Faith: We are saved by grace through faith but the manifestation of the gift of faith helps us to operate in new levels of boldness.

Healings: The power of God through you to deliver healings of all kinds to others.

Miracles: An act (or acts) of power demonstrating the power of the Holy Spirit. These are often connected to the gifts of healing and faith.

Discerning of spirits: Revelation regarding the specific power at work in someone's life or situation. This gift often partners with the gifts of knowledge and wisdom to know what to do with the revelation.

Different kinds of tongues: The supernatural ability to speak and pray in another language that you do not know. This can be done for the purposes of personal prayer to the Lord, in a gathering where the Lord uses another believer to interpret, and for evangelism where, without previous knowledge, the Holy Spirit enables you to speak in a native tongue that is understood by the hearers.

Interpretation of tongues: The ability to interpret the word given in public for the edification of the people.

There are also gifts such as the gift of administration, generosity, encouragement, teaching, mercy, and hospitality. You may have heard of these, in fact, you may already be aware and operating in your gifts. You also may have heard that some of these gifts don't exist anymore or that they are only reserved for certain people. I can tell you with confidence that the Lord wants you to encounter his power and love in ways that embolden and empower you. 1 Thessalonians 5:19 says, "Do not stifle the Holy Spirit." He has so much to reveal to you and he is at work doing that right now.

Goo or Good

As you learn more about the gifts and power of the Holy Spirit, does it intrigue you? Reading through this list, are you a bit freaked out? It is natural to be nervous or apprehensive when it comes to surrendering to the Holy Spirit. The aversion to the filling and operating in the power of the Holy Spirit is often related to the strange behavior and the stigma of being a weirdo. It takes great risk!

What does it look like to live a life filled and powered by God? First, I want you to know it's going to look like you—the powerful, free, beautiful version of you. God loves who you are! You are a delight to him. As you grow and experience the movement and presence of God you will come to desire that above the opinions and approval of others. In worship, there is often a freedom or inhibition that comes with the power of the Holy Spirit. People often sing, dance, shout, speak in tongues, cry, lay on the ground, or even shake. Do people fake this stuff? Probably some. Does that make it fake? No. Is it authentic and real for most? Yes. Is it worth it? Absolutely! These aren't bad things, but they may be past your comfort zone. That's okay!

The manifestations of the Spirit are strange because they are supernatural. If you've never experienced anything like this, it's okay to be apprehensive or nervous. I remember being nervous to raise my hands in worship. Now, you can't stop me! I begin to sing and my whole body responds to the majesty of God. My arms shoot up, or my hands clutch my heart, tears often stream down my face, and I abandon all cares. My Jesus is worth my highest praise! I also remember when I slowly began to allow myself to speak in tongues more often. I received that gift when I was thirteen years old at a youth service, but I never really did it again until I was in my thirties. I was afraid and unsure. Now, I speak in tongues all the time! It blesses my heart so much to let my soul groan to the Lord. It fills in the blanks where I can't possibly be eloquent enough to express my love, gratitude, intercession, or even sorrow to my King. I trust that the Holy Spirit is moving through me and accomplishing all that I can't on my own.

While the gifts of the Spirit are supernatural, we do partner with them. To speak in tongues, you need to move your mouth and make a sound. In order to give a word of knowledge to someone, you need to take a risk. To be used by the Lord to bring healing to someone, you need to ask if you can pray for them. It's all a risk. I've heard it said, God's gift to us is ability, our gift to Him is our availability. The more we make ourselves available with a yes to his leadership and empowerment, the easier it gets.

Just like any other gift, it takes practice, sacrifice, commitment, and dedication.

It may sound risky, and it is. Salvation is free but following Jesus will cost you everything. Jesus said it himself, when we lay down our lives and ourselves, we find life (Luke 8:25-27, Matthew 10:39). When we say yes to Jesus, we call him Lord of our lives. This means that we honor and worship God above all, not our comfort, our preferences, our agenda, or our desires. Our bodies are the temple of the Holy Spirit, and when we surrender to his leading and power, amazing things happen. From my experience of risking looking like a fool to pray for a stranger, giving a word of knowledge, stepping out in faith, and praying in a language that I do not know, is all worth it. The goodness and glory of God revealed to me and shown to others far surpasses my fear or ego.

But wait there's more

My husband and I have adopted a rule for ourselves. No more buffets. They look good and prey on my inner glutton, but they are so disappointing. We pay a lot of money to try all the foods that have been laid out to overwhelm your eyes, but the joy ends there. It's not nearly as tasty as it looks. In fact, most of the time it's downright gross! Plus, we can never eat as much as we imagine. We sample all the foods, don't like any of them enough to get more, and before we know it, we are full on a lot of subpar food. And don't get me started on the desserts. All looks, no flavor. Gross. We have done this one too many times, leading us to our now hard and fast rule.

If you haven't caught on by now, I have a bit of an inner glutton. I want more! While I have worked hard to not let that quality wreak havoc in unhealthy ways, there is something I can indulge in with positive effects. It's what I love about the Kingdom of

Heaven, there is always more. God is a gracious and loving Father who gives good gifts to his children. When it comes to the love of God and the blessings he bestows on us, there is no limit! Scripture says that the Spirit gives a gift to each believer so we can all contribute to helping others (1 Corinthians 12:7). We are given specifics according to what the Holy Spirit desires. I know from personal experience that we are not limited to one gift nor are they exclusive to only certain people. We can have as much as we want of the Lord and his goodness. I strongly believe that God, in his timing and grace, will allow us to experience his power in limitless ways. When it comes to the gifts of the Spirit, I am a spiritual hog because I want them all!

Gift of love

Gifts are just that—gifts. Scripture says that these cannot be taken away. We are free to use, misuse, or never use these gifts. That's the beauty of the love of God. We are always free to choose. It's a risk to give us that kind of power! In order to be good stewards of the gifts, it's vital that we care just as much about the cultivation of fruit in our lives as we do about the power of the gifts. We tend to place people on a pedestal, giving them the glory instead of Jesus. This is an extremely dangerous cycle. There has been much wounding in the body of Christ because too many people have been blinded by the attention and crushed by the weight of authority. Often, people become enamored by the package instead of grateful to the giver. Jesus says we will be known by our fruits, not our gifts. The enemy wants us to take the power and authority given to us by God and run off with it—using it for our own gain and leaving a wake of hurt beyond.

The core value of spiritual gifts is love. Paul makes that clear in 1 Corinthians 13 when he says if there is no love, they are all useless! It's the love that endures. It's love that makes them a gift. We need to be discerning when not only operating in the power of the Spirit through the spiritual gifts, but also as we are on the receiving end of the gifts. We must be on the lookout for love.

The best way to receive a gift is to test it. I love 1 Thessalonians 5:21, "Test everything that is said. Hold on to what is good." If you receive a word that doesn't sit well in your spirit or you just aren't sure it's true, put it on the shelf. Give it time. Write it down and wait for the Lord to reveal more. When someone steps out in faith to heal or give a word of knowledge and encouragement, it helps to be less focused on the results and more aware of the love. When we receive the love behind the word or the action, we will always walk away with a gift.

Double-sided grace

There really are no words to sufficiently thank the Lord for the grace and mercy we receive from the work of Jesus on the cross. We have been given the gift of grace that covers all our sins—past, present, and future. The word "grace" is typically defined as "unmerited favor." It's something we don't deserve but are given anyway because of God's unmatched love. While this gift gives us great freedom, it is not intended to be abused by living in such a way that says, "I can do whatever I want because I know I'm forgiven."

The Greek word for grace is *charis*, which is also the word for power. *Charismata* is the gift of power from the Holy Spirit. 2 Corinthians 12:9 says: "My grace is all you need. My power works best in weakness.' So now I am glad to boast about my weaknesses, so that the power of Christ can work through me." It's not often we find ourselves boasting about our weakness, but when we recognize it, we position ourselves to draw on God's power. The grace of God is like a double-sided coin. One side is the covering of favor, forgiveness, and love. The other side is the power we have because of the presence of the Holy Spirit to live like Jesus.

Too often we get caught up in the muck of what we can and can't do, what we should and shouldn't do. We tend to focus on what everyone else is up to and become the sin police. All of the worry and judgement about what is or isn't allowed or permitted just ties us up in knots and funnels our energy in the wrong direction. Paul addresses this issue in Romans 14:17, "For the Kingdom of God is not a matter of what we eat or drink, but of living a life of goodness and peace and joy in the Holy Spirit." When we are filled, surrendered to the Holy Spirit, and living in the power we receive, we ain't got time for all of that!

You may be new to the gifts, never consciously using them, but I can guarantee that there is at least one that you have already been given and used. Maybe you are aware of your gift(s) and have even leaned in, surrendering to the leading of the Holy Spirit. Great! I challenge you to ask and receive more! The Lord wants to bless you abundantly. He wants to give you good gifts that build you up and increase your knowledge of him. He has marvelous wonders to show you and to accomplish through you.

JOY BRINGER CHALLENGE

Joy in the box: A three-part visual and creative exercise.

I love this one! It's very powerful. There is no strict formula, but I am going to give you an outline and sample words to say if you would like to use them. You are free to let the Holy Spirit lead you and let Jesus do what he does best. It may help to read through each step so you know what's about to happen, or take it one step at a time.

PART ONE

Picture a large, empty box in front of you. Now is your time to put all the junk you don't want any more in that box. As things come to mind, say it aloud. Examples: "I put fear in the box. I put shame in the box. I put (addiction) in the box. I put (cruel nickname) in the box." Do it until you can't think of anything else. There is no such thing as running out of room or not putting enough in the box. You are free and there is no right or wrong way to do it.

PART TWO

Once your box is full of the junk, invite Jesus to come stand before you. This is your opportunity to give Jesus everything in your box. Ask him to take it from you. It's also a great opportunity to repent for placing any of those things above him in your life, or for any pain and suffering those things have caused others. Then, ask him to do something with your box, and watch what he does! You can use these words:

Jesus, I am giving you my box. I don't want it anymore. I am sorry for the times I've chosen these things over you. I am sorry for the hurt I've caused others and myself because of what's in here. I am done identifying with the junk in this box. I want to be rid of the stuff in this box. I am done with the pain it's caused. I know you are bigger than the stuff in here and I am asking you to take this box from me. Take it and do something with it. Do something that only you can do and show me what you do with my box. I trust you and I am grateful that you receive this and rid me of it with great joy!

PART THREE

Once Jesus has done something to your box, tell him how grateful you are. Thank him for his goodness and his love, but don't stop there! Ask Jesus to give you a gift in exchange for giving up your box. The Lord loves to give good gifts to his children, *and* he loves to make a great exchange. Read the prayer model below or make it your own and just talk to Jesus! Here is the prayer model:

Jesus, thank you for taking my box! Thank you for (how he got rid of it). You are so good! You are so powerful, and I declare that it's finished. I am done with those things! Help me, Holy Spirit, to stay free and to remember this moment. Jesus, in exchange for my box, will you give me something in return? I am asking for a gift, something that you want me to have to strengthen me, bring me joy, and fill me with wonder and love. Thank you for your generosity, I receive your gift!

_____

_____

_____

_____

_____

_____

_____

_____

_____

_____

Chapter 14:

Joy Bringer's Core Value–Flexibility

Joy verse

"Since we are living by the Spirit, let us follow the Spirit's
leading in every part of our lives."–Galatians 5:25 NLT

Being in very close proximity to orca whales. Not being able to get
a wad of gum out of my mouth. Having to choose between two
people to marry. Running out of a movie theater with monsters
chasing me. These are just a few of the recurring dreams I've had
throughout my life. They are quite fascinating. While not all
dreams are prophetic or from the Lord, God loves to speak to us
through dreams and visions. In fact, one third of the Bible is made
up of dreams or visions. We spend one third of our lives sleeping
so it's a great opportunity to hear from the Lord!

One of my more enjoyable recurring dreams is that I am very
flexible. In my dream I am stretching or doing the splits, but I
can't reach the limit of my flexibility. I wake up and wish that I
had that kind of mobility and freedom in my body. And believe it
or not, God wants a version of that for us too. That's why the third
Joy Bringer's Core Value is flexibility.

The very nature of the Holy Spirit is fluid and free. Wind, fire, and water are all things that move without limits. All things that, in nature, are uncontainable. Living a life filled with the Spirit means we are available to move with the Spirit. This means loosening our grip of control and following the leading of the Lord whose plans and ways are higher than our view and often, our understanding. "We can make our plans, but the Lord determines our steps" (Proverbs 16:9).

My grandmother was a professional dancer. She was petite but strong. She would dance with my grandfather who was almost a foot taller than her but together they moved as one. The Lord wants to dance with us, not strongarm us or force us into submission. As we grow to trust the goodness of the Lord, we become more adept at following his lead. We learn the subtle and sometimes not so subtle invitations to change tempo, direction, and even style. Change is inevitable and if we don't bend we will break.

If you don't like change, I have good news for you: God's love is steadfast and never changing. He is faithful and will never fail. We can trust that the character and nature of the Lord was, is, and always will be the same. Words like rock, fortress, oak tree, and mountain are used to describe the Lord and his nature. These words convey strength and might, stability and protection, but that doesn't mean that the Lord doesn't move.

The enemy loves to use fear to keep us from moving. We develop a tight grip of control on people and things around us because we believe that it is safer for our hearts. It has even become socially acceptable to wear the badge and proclaim, "I'm a control freak." Self-control is faith in the Lord to meet our needs and satisfy our souls. Control is the opposite of trust and rooted in fear. It keeps us rigid—unable to bend, and after enough pressure, we break. Flexibility, moving with the Spirit, helps protect us and maintain our joy.

In my mid-twenties I had everything I thought I wanted. A successful career as an actor, a husband, a house, an amazing family and group of friends. But things quickly fell apart. My grandmother died a few weeks after I was married. Thirty days into my marriage, my husband cheated on me with my best friend. One month after that my mom died. Within a very short time, I went from being the baby of my family to the matriarch because my mother, both grandmothers, and two great aunts passed within a short span of each other. My first husband and I bought a home at the height of the housing bubble. I lost my husband to divorce and my house to the recession at the same time. All the things I thought were secure in my life were not. The only thing left was my career.

"I will die on this stage." I said that and meant it. In the height of my performing career my desire was to be a part of the theatre company I worked for until I was too old to stand or remember my lines. I couldn't imagine life any different. Building success and satisfaction around a group of people or an organization didn't seem like a bad thing. I was committed and passionate, that was a good thing. Right? It was all I felt I had left, and I was going to hold on tight.

As I was healing from the trauma and pain of immense loss, I began to desire something different. My greatest desire became following Jesus. I began to pray every day, "Whatever, wherever." I had no idea what that would mean or where it would lead but I told the Lord, "I lived my dream, so I want you to dream for me now. I will do whatever you have for me and go wherever you lead."

I loosened my grip and opened my eyes and ears to the movement of the Spirit. I had grand visions of giving up everything and becoming a nun in Timbuktu, whatever would be the most dramatic and selfless act of surrender for the Lord. Clearly, that's not what happened. But where the Holy Spirit did lead me was to seminary, Christinamingle.com, and eventually to another city to become a wife and an insta-mom. Losing my grip on my life and the way I had it planned opened me up to so much more than I could have imagined. Surrendering to the Lord and following his lead didn't mean suffering and scarcity. It meant abundance and beauty beyond what I imagined possible.

Following Jesus and being surrendered to the leading of the Holy Spirit doesn't necessarily mean we need to undergo a major career change, sell everything we own, or move to a different city. God simply wants us to be available. He wants to use us to accomplish his great work and in order to do that it means staying attentive and willing, loosening our grip, and being flexible.

The first command

A plaque that hung in my parents' bedroom had the Ten Commandments written on it. The first line read, "Thou shalt not have any other gods before me." I never understood that one as a child. I remember reading them all and thinking, "I'm doing pretty good! I don't steal, haven't committed murder, I don't bow down to statues. I guess I could do better at the honoring my parents part, and I don't know what coveting is so I guess I'm good there too." It wasn't until I was much older that I learned how we so easily do worship other gods.

Money, sex, and stuff most often become the things to which we bow down. It's pretty easy to figure out what we idolize just by checking our bank statements and calendars. What takes priority in our lives? In our ego-centric, self-involved, consumer-driven culture we often place our own interests, desires, achievement, and satisfaction over our desire for the Lord.

It's not easy to examine this part of our lives. It threatens our comfort. Especially in America where we will fight to the death if we feel our security or freedom being threatened. The reality is it's not our freedom or security that is in danger, we've just built an altar to our preferences and justified our worship. But there are also idols dressed up in righteous clothing. Idols such as:

- Placing our identities in our role as parents. "My kids are my life."
- Serving in church at the sacrifice of our mental, physical, emotional, and spiritual health. "Serving the Lord is my priority; my family will understand."
- Being so impassioned for a cause that those on the other side of the debate become hated enemies. "(Fill in the blanks) can go to hell."

No matter how "good" our intentions are, we must be aware of our tendency to make God in our preferred image. We value comfort over risk. We value tradition over change. We want things to stay the same because it's what we know. Without realizing it, we have given those things golden calf status in our lives and bow down in worship.

God isn't trying to control you. That's not love. And he doesn't want us to be under the control of anyone or anything else. Jesus came to give us abundant life and freedom, not to be enslaved to sin and limited by our narrow vision. God's goodness and faithfulness will never fail us. He is worthy of our trust and devotion. Scripture says, "For the Lord is the Spirit, and wherever the Spirit of the Lord is, there is freedom" (2 Corinthians 3:17). The Holy Spirit doesn't belong in a cage or a box. God wants you to be free from bondage. When we surrender our control and agenda and trust the leading of the Lord, amazing things happen!

I dare you

In a game of truth or dare, I always pick truth. I would rather be honest than risky. Plus, there is no prize in that game! Doing something embarrassing for no reason? No, thank you. But I have learned to trust the nudge of the Lord and take the risk because the rewards far outweigh the risk.

As I was practicing hearing from the Lord and surrendering to his lead, I told God, "I will look like a fool for you. If I hear it or sense it, I will say it or do it." This has led me to some really awkward moments, and also really beautiful ones. The first major risk I took was on an airplane. I was reading a great book about prophecy (*You May All Prophesy* by Steve Thompson) and I was ready to step it up. I wanted to allow the Holy Spirit to speak encouragement and love to others through me. I couldn't shake the vision I had of a giant engagement ring over the man's head who was sitting across the aisle from me. It was huge! A large solitaire diamond. I assumed it was an engagement ring.

The man had large headphones on and was working on his computer for most of the flight, so the moment he took his headphones off, shut his computer and got up to go to the bathroom, I knew I had my chance. When he returned to his seat I spoke to him. Our conversation went like this:

"Excuse me, are you engaged?"

"No" he said.

"Well, are you thinking about getting engaged?"

"No" he said again.

"Well, I don't know if you believe in God, but I see an engagement ring over you. I wanted you to know the Lord loves you and sees you."

"I'm not engaged, in fact I have two different girlfriends in two different countries. One of them is picking me up at the airport."

Shocked and almost speechless, I said something nice and let him go back to his work. I was so embarrassed! I went back to my book, pretending to read while silently praying, "Lord! I tried and I failed! I thought I had it right! Now he thinks I am an idiot, and he didn't get a revelation of your love." The Lord stopped my woe-is-me rant and said, "You have no idea what just happened. It's not for you to worry about." He was right! It wasn't about me. I didn't do any harm or speak anything other than love. So what if my ego took a hit? I was going to trust that God would take my measly offering of risk and faith and use it for good. What if, at the airport when he got into the car of girlfriend number one, she gave him an ultimatum. Perhaps she said, "We get engaged or we're done!" Or, what if someday when he does go to buy a ring for someone, he remembers that God loves him?

It wasn't any of my business what God was going to do with my offering. No matter what, he's worth the sacrifice. God has chosen me and you to be his hands and feet. We get to be bearers of good news to those we meet. What an honor! We have been given a part to play, not the responsibility of the outcome. That's freeing!

It's fun

Have you ever randomly become aware of tension in your jaw and shoulders and realized you are holding your breath? It happens to us many times a day! Too often we are tense, full of stress and doing our best to hold on. But what if we let go? What if, instead of squeezing tighter we opened our hands? What if, instead of needing to have a plan and control all the details, we trusted the Lord to lead the way? I am not saying that preparing and planning are bad. It is certainly honoring to the Lord and those around you, but they become a hindrance when we don't leave room for the Spirit.

God loves new things. He's always up to something new and good. Change is certain in this world. If we are going to keep in step with the Lord, we must make flexibility a core value. Not the kind that helps us touch our toes (although that is extremely healthy for us). We need the kind of flexibility that helps us live full of joy. Moving with the Spirit takes courage and risk, but it is more fulfilling and even more fun than breaking from our rigidity due to fear and stubbornness.

If Jesus is the original joy bringer, the Holy Spirit is the joy maker. In the presence of the Lord is joy! God loves fun, whimsy, beauty, laughter, and freedom. If the idea of flexibility and change freaks you out, I bless you to know that God isn't trying to cause you harm by inviting you to become more flexible. Look around! There is creativity, humor, and delight everywhere. God wants you to experience more of these things! He wants you to maintain joy, to stay loose and available to enjoy his goodness.

JOY BRINGER CHALLENGE

Speaking of the game Truth or Dare, I challenge you to a game! **TRUTH**: What are you holding onto with an iron grip?
- Family
- Money
- Career
- Reputation
- Sin
- Possessions
- Location
- Friends

Are you ready to loosen your grip? Let's surrender our fear to the Lord and trust him with our hearts.

DARE: I dare you to step out of your comfort zone this week (or today!). Ask the Lord to lead you then follow him! That may mean you feel an urge to call someone to pray for them or leave a note with some money at a gas station. You may have a strange word or vision that might not make sense to you, but you know it's for someone else. Tell them! It could also mean that you take some time alone and let the Spirit fill your mouth as you pray in tongues for the first time. The Lord has a good gift for you, receive it! Take it out of the box and use it!

Take a moment to test the level of flexibility in your life. Answer these questions:

- Are there things in your life that are currently off-limits to change?
- Is the schedule or agenda on the throne of your life or church?
- How do you react when things change?
- What are some ways you could begin to loosen up to the movement of the Spirit?

_____

_____

_____

_____

_____

_____

_____

_____

_____

Section 4: Leading

Joy verse:

"The joy of the Lord is your strength!"–Nehemiah 8:10 NLT

Joy Principle:

Don't be strong, be joyful!

Core value:

Rest

Being an actor is not as glamorous as it seems. It's a very bizarre life, and especially strange in acting school. I remember many phone conversations with my mother that went something like this:

Mom: "What did you do in class today, honey?"

Me: "Well, in my voice and movement class we were interacting with each other as our favorite weather pattern."

Mom: "Oh! What weather pattern were you?"

Me: "A bright sunny day and I was having a conversation with a tornado."

There were times in acting class when I would perform a monologue in gibberish, or my scene partner and I would be animals instead of people. The sights and sounds coming from inside an acting class were always intriguing, leaving anyone outside who heard us wondering, "What *are* they doing in there?!"

The goal in playing a role was to create a real, multidimensional character, not just a talking head. We would do exercises to explore how our bodies are connected to our emotions and personalities. One in particular started with us walking naturally in a circle around the room. The professor instructed us to choose a certain body part to lead with, exaggerating the movement to the extreme. We would walk with our hips pushed out in front of us, or our necks stretched out with our noses leading the way. The professor would then ask us to lessen the intensity of the movement to a more natural state. Depending on what the person was leading from, a character could be born. Perhaps one with their nose protruding would be someone who was snooty and above the rest, or another might be a detective searching a room to discover the location of a certain smell. The person leading with their hips might be a sultry woman trying to get attention, or a pregnant woman ready to pop.

What we lead with informs much about us. My desire in this section is to help you lead your life with joy. So far, we've begun to realize the magnitude of the good news of salvation, embarked on a healing journey, and encountered and been empowered by the Holy Spirit. Now it's time to be led by joy into the world. Jesus commissioned us to take that good news and go. But wait, there's more good news, we're not meant to do it alone! But going out into the world means facing many challenges. I want to help you walk through the challenges of adversity and pain with confidence in the ever-present love and protection of Jesus.

Two in one

Most people would agree that a leader needs to be strong. Leadership is challenging and not for the faint of heart. But where we've missed the boat is that we have looked to just about everything else to find or gain strength when all along, the greatest source of strength is found in the joyful presence of Jesus. Joy and strength are not mutually exclusive, they are partners! The Lord wants us to be strengthened by his power and filled with his joy so we can lead ourselves and others with joy.

Chapter 15:

Leading from joy

Joy verse

"So you'll go out in joy, you'll be led into a whole and complete life."–Isaiah 55:12 MSG

"As I lay me down to sleep…" I hated that prayer when I was younger. My Grandma used to say it with me when I would spend the night at her house. The words, "If I should die before I wake, I pray the Lord my soul to take" freaked me out! I would lay in bed thinking about how I didn't want to die. I hadn't had the chance to get my driver's license or get married! Now when I lay in bed at night, most often I think about what's on the docket for the next day. Is it fun? Will I enjoy it? How can I avoid what I don't want to do? Will it take everything I have to get out of bed, go through the motions and not lose my mind? Then I think about the liquid glory that I will consume moments after my feet hit the floor in the morning and suddenly *that* joy overrides whatever is on the schedule. It's very clear by now that while I am fueled by the sweet, hot, creamy goodness in a large mug with a straw every morning, I also lead from joy.

Everyone leads their lives from something and what we lead from informs a lot about us. We often lead with our knowledge and expertise, our charm and smile, or threat and aggression. What do you lead from? What is it that informs and powers your life every day? When we leave it up to our circumstances and the people around us, we are tossed and blown by the winds of change. The key is to wake up every day to the good news that never changes: "So you'll *go out in joy*, you'll be led into a whole and complete life" (Isaiah 55:12 MSG. emphasis added). Yup, that's the goal! That's why we have been on this journey, but it takes intentionality.

Jesus led from joy. The good news was announced at his birth. The joy he knew powered him through his life and ministry. He told people again and again that there was great joy in living in relationship with the Father and in doing his will. It was joy that sent Jesus out to heal and proclaim the truth. It was joy that helped Jesus endure the cross. His joy was powerful and contagious, and people wanted to follow him. Jesus valued his joy, so he protected it. He made strong choices to maintain it and so can you.

Choose joy

When I was a student in middle school, best friend necklaces were all the rage. Wearing half of a heart that said either "Be Fri" or "St Ends" meant that you were joined in the sanctified union of best friendship with someone (or often, many). One day, a girl who wore the "st ends" to my "be fri" gave me back her half. She told me she had a new "be fri" and I was devastated. That new girl stole my best friend! Through sobs I explained to my mom what had happened, and she told me something that stuck. "No one has the power to steal another person from you. She made a choice." While it didn't really help the pain, it opened my eyes to the truth: Our choices are powerful.

No one and nothing has the power to steal your joy if it's rooted in Jesus. However, we can make the choice to let it go or give it away. We are powerful people. We have the power to choose. How we live our life matters. What we invest in matters. The choices we make every day have a great impact on our joy. What we watch, listen to, speak, and do contributes to either maintaining our focus on Jesus and filling us with joy and life or leading us down a road that ends in death.

Jesus didn't live in a bubble. He lived in the real world. While things are faster and more technologically advanced in the twenty-first century, the same basic needs and temptations still exist. Jesus had to make the same kinds of choices we do today. But because he stayed so connected to his Father and drew from the pure goodness and abundance of heaven, he was able to stay free from the bondage of sin.

My husband hates seaweed but loves the ocean. The feeling of seaweed tangled around his legs is enough for him to get out and stay out. Just like the slimy reeds that wrap around your legs, the writer of Hebrews (a book in The Bible) describes sin as something that so easily entangles, and just like that seaweed, it robs us from the good stuff. Life is already full of challenges so it's vital that we set ourselves up for success by recognizing the threats to our joy and choosing to set up intentional guardrails in our lives to protect it.

Danger ahead

There is a reason danger zones have bright yellow caution tape around them. They are dangerous! Only you know what areas are danger zones in your life. Everyone has them but powerful people (that's you!) recognize them and make efforts to avoid them. No one is immune from temptation, even Jesus was tempted. Temptation isn't a sin, but we cross the line when we grab hold of the offer. That's when we give away our joy.

I got a call from a friend of mine. She said, "Hi, I was reaching for the phone to call him, and I know that talking to him isn't good for either of us, so I am calling you. Can you chat?" I was so proud of her! That's the way to do it. Recognizing the danger zones and having a plan to make a safe detour. While we were on the phone, we talked about why she had the desire to call this person. She recognized the trigger and we got to the root. She was avoiding feeling certain emotions she needed to process. Oh man can I relate! If we aren't careful, our efforts to escape can lead us straight into the danger zone.

A big danger zone for me is striving and losing my identity in my work. For most of my life I identified as an actor. It wasn't just what I did, it was who I was. When I retired from that career, I felt lost. I cried out to the Lord, "If I'm not an actor, who am I?!" Without missing a beat, he said, "You are mine." Shortly after, I had those words tattooed on my wrist. While those words are the truest thing about me, I still struggle to keep my identity rooted in who he says I am and not what job I am doing. Recognizing it as a danger zone helps me to hold onto my joy as a daughter of the King and not give it away to the next job title.

Jesus will never lead us into sin. We always have the Holy Spirit with us as a guide. Let's read what Psalm 16:11 (NIV) says about our guide: "You make known to me the path of life; you will fill me with joy in your presence, with eternal pleasures at your right hand." The path of life and joy is the antithesis of the danger zone that is full of entanglement, pain, and death. When we stay in step with Jesus and in tune with the Holy Spirit, we choose joy.

Core values are key

When I met Christina, I was immediately intrigued by her. She was bold, powerful, and always joyful. We were on a leadership team together and had an opportunity to travel as a team to connect and be inspired. As we piled in the car to head to the airport, she handed each of us a piece of paper. On it were a list of her core values with an explanation and example of each, including biblical references. She said, "If we are going to be in a relationship and work together, I need you to know who I am and what I stand for. Please read these. I am asking you to hold me accountable." Wow! Who does that? Christina does. A woman who is indeed bold, powerful, trustworthy, and joyful.

Christina is not perfect. She never claimed to be. But she knew the value of joy in Jesus, and she set up her life in a way to maintain that joy. What made her trustworthy was her transparency and commitment to live by a set of values made known to those around her. We would come to expect certain behaviors or responses from her because we knew what she stood for. She was approachable and humble, and her joy and laughter were contagious. I wanted to be like Christina, so I made a list of core values too.

Core values answer the questions before they arise. If one of your core values is to live debt-free, then you already know if you don't have the money in the bank for that new TV, you aren't buying it. If you have established a core value of transparency, when there is temptation to hide or cover something up, you choose to expose it right away. If rest is a core value, then you won't be a 'yes' machine filling every waking hour with meetings, tasks, taxiing your family around, and attending events. Instead, you'll be the master of your own schedule giving your best yes and your kind but firm no, intentionally making room for rest.

Core values are for everyone and every situation. When we set up these guardrails in our life, we help to protect our joy. My husband and I have our own individual core values and a set for our marriage. Knowing my husband's core values has helped me understand him. Much like love languages, understanding what's behind my husband's decisions helps me support him (even when I don't hold the same values). When you come together as a team, family, business, or church to create and agree on core values then everyone knows what's important and what to expect. Everyone has a hand in protecting and maintaining joy.

JOY BRINGER CHALLENGE

If you haven't already established a set of core values for yourself, I challenge you to start now. Identify four to six (too many can be overwhelming or confusing), write them down and elaborate on them. Include why they are each important to you, give examples of what they look like, and include scriptural references (if they apply).

Here is an example from one of my personal core values.

Quick obedience: I value the leading and instruction of the Lord. When I hear the Lord's voice, I will obey quickly. Too often in my life I have ignored the voice of the Spirit and due to my own pride, stubbornness, laziness, and fear I have been hurt and hurt others. Quick obedience is not only about sin, it's about opportunity. I don't want to miss what the Lord has for me! It looks like going to someone when I have been wrong or unkind and apologizing. Hearing a word of encouragement or feeling the nudge to pray for someone and doing it immediately before I forget or allow doubt and fear to deter me. The Bible says in Psalm 119:2,

"Joyful are those who obey his laws and search for him with all their hearts."

Here is a brief list of core values. This is in no way a complete list; ask the Lord to highlight some or inspire you with others.

Authenticity	Forgiveness*	Meaningful work
Achievement	Freedom	Openness
Adventure	Friendships	Organization
Awareness	Fun	Optimism
Balance	Generosity	Peace
Beauty	Gratitude*	Pleasure
Boldness	Growth	Poise
Compassion	Happiness	Recognition
Challenge	Helpfulness	Respect
Citizenship	Honesty	Responsibility
Community	Honor	Rest*
Competence	Humor	Security
Contribution	Influence	Self-Respect
Creativity	Integrity	Service
Curiosity	Intimacy	Simplicity
Discover	Justice	Spirituality
Dependability	Kindness	Stability
Determination	Knowledge	Success
Earth care	Leadership	Transparency
Fairness	Learning	Trustworthy
Faith	Legacy	Warmth
Fitness	Love	Wealth
Flexibility*	Loyalty	Wisdom

*Joy Bringer's core values

Once you've chosen a few core values, established what they mean to you, as well as what they would look like in your life, bring them to your loved ones. Ask them if the values you've chosen are in line with who you are, and if there may be some you're missing. Remember, core values aren't just to help you maintain your joy, they benefit those around you as well.

Chapter 16:

Complete Joy

Joy verse
"We write this to make our joy complete."
–1 John 1:4 NIV

"You look so good today! Your eyes are sparkling, and your smile lights up the room! You're amazing!" If you heard that before you started each day, you might walk out the door with your head held high and maybe keep paying forward the encouragement and kindness to everyone you meet. Unfortunately, those are not the words we often hear in our heads as our morning self-talk. But those are the kinds of words the Lord says over you. Right now, he is looking at you with delight and love in his eyes. He has wonderful things to say to you and he wants his words and love to fill you with joy so you will lead with joy.

Without realizing it, we often believe that God looks at us with anger or disapproval, or that he doesn't look at us at all, out of sight out of mind. But because of Jesus, the Father sees you covered in his righteousness. He sees you as his beautiful, unique creation, redeemed by the blood of his son, full of power and purpose. He also sees your neighbor, archrival, and enemy the same way. And he wants you to see yourself (and them) that was as well.

The older I get, the more love I have for people. I feel a bit silly sometimes. I look at someone and could just burst into tears with love and compassion for them. But this wasn't always the case. In the past I've said things like, "I can't stand women, they're so annoying" and thought horrible things about those different from me. I am ashamed of the prejudice and disdain (albeit mostly hidden or subconscious) I've had toward others, and I pray that the Lord continues to uproot those things in me. My perspective really began to change as the Lord was healing me with his love. If God could see me through eyes of love, grace, mercy, and delight then I could try to see myself that way as well. When I exchanged my dark lenses of scrutiny, comparison, and hatred for his clear, truthful lenses I saw myself and others around me with new technicolor beauty!

Made for community

The Trinity: Father, Son, and Holy Spirit, existed before the world began. Before there was anything else, there was community. Their love for one another was so good it needed to be shared. Cue creation! Things were very good in the garden. Beautiful variety existed with harmony and unity, until division showed up. Fear and shame caused deceit and accusation which led to isolation and sides were created.

Those people. It's the category of people who are not like you. The ones on the wrong side. We all have them. If you don't think you do, who would you *not* like your college-age child to bring home and say, "We're getting married!" Or who would qualify as the worst prospective neighbor? It could be a certain race, a socio-economic class, one who identifies in a way you don't understand, a political affiliation, or even people from your past. There aren't any limits to the qualifications of the other.

Prejudice and disdain isn't easy to admit. I believe most people earnestly want to say they love and accept everyone, but unfortunately, we all have hidden (and sometimes not so hidden) hatred toward the other. As hard as that is to swallow that is what it is, hatred.

We are made in the image of God, a God that exists in community. We were created by love, for love, with joy, for joy. This means that being in community with others is a part of our original design. I want to remind us that while we are whole beings in of ourselves, we are meant to make up a collective being—united as one body with many parts. Catch that. Many parts, not all the same parts. Not all the same gifts, looks, personalities, styles, languages, colors, and thoughts. This requires us to do some "other" work.

Each member of the Trinity is quite different but honors and loves the other. Jesus isn't threatened by the Holy Spirit. He longed for the world to experience his power and goodness. The Father isn't jealous of Jesus. He delights in his son and his work and is glorified when we worship Jesus as King. On earth, people couldn't get enough of Jesus! Crowds of people clamored to get to him, but Jesus pointed them to his Father. The enemy knows he can't create division within the Trinity, so he's hard at work driving wedges of division through humanity. And he doesn't have to work that hard!

Who is your neighbor?

We've heard it many times, "Love your neighbor as yourself." That's super easy when you have a neighbor who, when you ask to borrow a ladder to clean your gutters, instead sends her son to joyfully do it for you (I'm looking at you, April). But what about "those neighbors," the ones who aren't so easy to love? The ones whose very existence seems to revolve around making your life difficult or disturbed. From what we've learned about love, it's not just to tolerate or ignore, it's selfless action that looks like Jesus.

Who is your neighbor? The definition isn't limited to those who live on your block or in your building. When Jesus is asked this question, he shares the story of the Good Samaritan. Of course, he didn't give this story a title, so his listeners didn't know what was about to hit them because those words were an oxymoron. The story goes that a man was walking from Jerusalem to Jericho when he was attacked and left for dead in the middle of the road. The first two people to approach the man, a priest and a Levite (both religious elite) ignored him. But it was the third, a Samaritan, who stopped to help the man, going above and beyond to care for his needs.

This was a deep burn to the religious hearers. The Samaritan was considered a half-breed, an outcast. They were not considered part of the community of God. Therefore, the assumption was that nothing good would come from them. The priest and Levite would have been too concerned with the laws of purity to risk their own contamination, so they chose to ignore the man in need instead of doing good. The man who was hurt was a Jew, but his own people didn't care enough to help him. Jesus told his listeners to be like the Samaritan, to love and care for those who are not only in your community but those who are outside, the "others," if you will.

We must catch another vital point of this story. We don't need to worry about helping those we've deemed "unclean." The way Jesus loved and spent time with those outside the elite purity club really ticked people off. We often act as if people's sin is contagious and stay far away. Don't get me wrong, it's important to be wise and not put yourself in a position where temptation is too strong, but loving a neighbor well requires us to be with them. Love speaks through our time, proximity, words, resources, and efforts.

One of my favorite things Tyler Merritt (of the Tyler Merritt Project) says is, "Proximity breads empathy." From afar we can size up and assume all manner of things about someone. But up close we find we are more similar than different. But getting close is a risk! "What will people think?!" It's an age-old question. For the sake of love, Jesus didn't care what the religious elite thought of his dinner guests or who he walked with. Paul confidently shared in 1 Corinthians 9 that for the sake of sharing the love of Jesus he wasn't afraid to live among and be like the Jews or the gentiles.

But before we get all high and mighty, let's remember that the Lord chose to come close to us first. God is holy. He is set apart in his perfection. He chooses to come near to us in our brokenness out of love, mercy, and compassion. No one is closer to us than the Lord. That's saying something. If proximity breads empathy, he understands us more than anyone, more than we understand ourselves. His loving kindness is closer than our breath and intended to fill us with courage. Our quest to love our neighbor will take us out of our comfort zones. We will meet people who are different and yet so similar. That's a good thing! The Lord has great intention to use you to reach the lost, broken and hurt, and he has wonderful plans for those you meet to be a blessing to you as well.

Lonely, party of one

For the first time in history there are actual governmental departments and roles being created to address the problem of loneliness across the globe. The often labeled, "Loneliness Epidemic" was around before COVID-19, but certainly exacerbated by the pandemic. Loneliness is not the same as being alone.

It's been determined that while loneliness is not the cause, it is directly related to many diseases and premature death. It's possible to be lonely in a marriage or family, in a large crowd of people, and with many "friends" on social media. Loneliness is a state of feeling disconnected from authentic community and lacking desired intimacy.

We live in a dichotomy. We want to be connected but at the same time we want freedom. We are told we can do anything we want, and no one can tell us who to be, but we lack the support or guidance of those who've gone before. Unlimited possibility seems great but inside we are dying of anxiety and overwhelmed by so many choices. People are longing for guidance and told to look inward because, "The answer lies within you." The more self-dependent we are, the more isolated we become. In our quest for confidence, success, and power, we have forgotten the adage, "If you want to go fast, go alone. If you want to go far, go together."

JOY BRINGER CHALLENGE

I challenge you to be a Joy Bringer and reach out to someone. The Lord will highlight someone you know who is lonely or even a stranger you see throughout your day. Do something. Say something. Anything! Your smile is powerful. Your words are life-giving. Your touch is healing. Your eye contact is important. A simple conversion, a note, a text, or invitation has the power to radically change someone's day, or even save a life.

If you are currently feeling lonely, I challenge you to make a phone call or show up to a gathering. Be intentional. The enemy wants you to spiral down the rabbit hole of lies that say you are not wanted, welcome, or liked. Not true! There are churches, community centers, neighbors, and even phone lines ready to connect with you.

Complete joy

My inner glutton is always up for more. So, when I read the words, "complete joy" in the New Testament, I'm intrigued. What is complete joy? How can I have not just more joy, but *complete* joy? Jesus mentions it, so does Paul, John, and Peter. Anytime complete joy is mentioned it is in reference to shared joy. Complete joy is joy shared in community. And that right there is why the enemy loves division. He may not be creative, but he's not stupid. He knows that joy is made complete in community, and he wants to keep us from the good stuff.

I went to Seminary with people of different ages, races, denominations, and worship style preferences. It was a beautiful community reminiscent of heaven. The faith journeys and stories in those classrooms were inspiring. While we had a colorful and rich diversity, we did not always have agreement. One of my professors said something so powerful it shifted my perspective on differences. "Not one denomination can fully encompass the glory of God." This same statement can be applied to many things. The glory of God is not captured or fully exhibited in one race, country, teaching or learning style, structure, or any one generation's set of ideas or ideals.

Scripture says that the mighty angelic creatures surrounding the throne of God have six wings and are covered with eyes. We only have two eyes (although moms do have that set of eyes in the back of their head) and we see so much. Imagine being *covered* in eyes. The perspective and detail would be overwhelming. With that many eyes, what do the angels see? Well, they never stop saying, "Holy, Holy, Holy is the Lord Almighty; the *whole earth* is full of his glory" (Isaiah 6:3 NIV, emphasis added by me). With the ability to see everything at once, the angels are overcome by the holiness of God and his glory that fills the entire earth. That's what it takes to even begin to understand the scope, eyes to see it everywhere, in everyone, in everything.

We need to stop thinking that our church, friend group, political party, region, country, race, or any other preference has the corner market on the truth or the goodness and glory of God. We miss out on so much beauty and revelation by insulating ourselves with those who share our ideas and preferences. God loves his unique and vast creation, and he is delighted to reveal himself even more to us when we are intentional to look.

Wounded healer

"Season the sea cow" was the nickname I acquired in the fourth grade when I did an oral report on the Manatee. The hurtful name hung on for a few years, but the pain lasted for decades. I was bullied in every school, even in my church youth group. There was always something used as a weapon. I changed elementary schools halfway through the third grade. It was discovered very quickly that a popular boy and I shared the same birthday. The collective hive decided that I loved him and wanted to marry him, which brought on relentless jeering and rumors. In both my high school and church youth group I was made fun of because of my talent and love of the theatre. While singing on the worship team at church, students would throw things at me and make fun of my passion and enthusiasm.

Cliques, bullying, and rejection aren't just reserved for the elementary school playground. Being hurt by people and organizations including the Church is often why many avoid, or even run from the thought of community. That's the goal of the enemy: to isolate us so that we walk around with our walls up, judgements and accusations at the ready. If he can keep us from authentic loving connection and unity, we miss experiencing the complete joy found in community.

JOYFUL DISCOVERY

Harmony is the combination of different notes played at the same time. Together the different notes make up a chord. Depending on how many notes and where they are in proximity to each other, the sound varies. An individual voice has its own beauty and value, but when combined with other unique voices, the experience is enriched, and the sound becomes fuller. Harmony is difference in unity.

Unity (not sameness) begins with the revelation that while our differences may seem vast, we are more similar than we realize. We all have scars. Even Jesus has scars! And we all need healing. When we experience the radical grace, mercy, and love from the Lord it changes the way we see ourselves and affects the way we see others.

So how do we achieve unity (not sameness or even agreement) in such a divided world? Once again, Jesus delivers this doozy: "Love your enemies and pray for those who persecute you" (Matthew 5:44 NIV). Odds are you've heard that one, but like most people, hit the decline button. It doesn't seem fair, does it? Why should *we* be the ones to pray for those we can't stand? *They* are the ones doing it wrong! So instead, we pray they will be hit with the wrath of God or that they will be converted to our way of thinking or living.

Jesus was well-acquainted with this challenge. Just as he was deeply loved, he was also deeply hated. But he too practiced what he preached, loving his enemies, and praying and forgiving those who persecuted him. Even on the cross, as an innocent man he prayed asking his Father to forgive his murderers. Imagine having compassion on the ones who are literally killing you!

This is a good time to remind us that it's not our job to "convert" or even "fix" anyone. Like the Good Samaritan, our calling is to love our neighbors and help those in need. It's the Holy Spirit that does the work of salvation, we get to do the work of bringing the goodness and joy to everyone we encounter and let God do the rest.

We need people. That may take time to wrap your brain around because we have been conditioned to not trust people and make it on our own. I want you to experience the *complete* joy the Lord has for you, and that is only found through community. I invite you to read these statements and see if there is any revelation the Lord may have for you regarding healing and welcoming community. These are the statements:

- You cannot love God and hate people. They are made in his image and are the jewel in the crown of his creation.
- Justice isn't fairness according to your perspective. The Lord sees not only every angle but knows our hearts and our motives.
- We have a two-way connection with the Lord, vertical and horizontal. The Lord reveals himself to us directly and *through* others.
- If everyone in your circle of friends thinks the same as you, looks like you, and connects with God the same way you do, what revelation of God's glory are you missing?

If any of these struck a chord (remember multiple notes working together), listen. Open your ears and heart to the Lord, he has goodness and joy to reveal to you. In the words of Jesus found in John 15:11 (NIV), "I have told you this so that my joy may be in you and that your joy may be complete."

JOY BRINGER CHALLENGE

I challenge you to love your neighbor this week. Start with your own block or building. Choose someone you've never had a connection with and do something to show them some love, kindness, or help.

Also, take a moment to ask the Lord to highlight "others" in your life. Ask him to show you his love for them and see if there is any opportunity for you to do a little Core Value work and forgive.

Chapter 17:

Joyful Leadership

Joy verse

"The joy of the Lord is your strength."–Nehemiah 8:10 NIV

For much of my life I didn't believe I was a leader. I thought, "I am a great number two." I loved to champion a vision and work with a team, but I didn't think I had what it took to be a real leader. I didn't look or act like the leaders I worked with. I figured I was too young, joyful, or dare I say it, female. As I have grown in my trust in the Lord, I have learned that I am called to lead. Just like you.

You don't have to own a business, have people serving you, or be a social media influencer to be a leader. We've been given the gift of freedom to lead our own lives anyway we want (within legal parameters) and because people are watching, the choices we make have a great impact not only on ourselves but on the lives of those around us. We lead people every day without even knowing it and people follow our lead whether we tell them to or not. With this revelation, it's important to take responsibility for our influence and be intentional to lead from joy and with great care.

It's a privilege to be given the authority to lead others. And it's vital that we are aware of our leadership style and methods. How we lead others matters. Are you a tyrant, commanding with no compassion? Are you busy and burdened, slammed and stressed to the max? Are you brilliant and isolated, leading without connection? Or are you a joyful leader who is passionate and inviting? Jesus, arguably the greatest leader to ever walk this planet, was joyful. We are invited to emulate him, leading from joy, and leading people to *the* Joy Bringer.

Joyful leader

Joy is not a quality typically found on the list of vital leadership characteristics. Most leaders are perceived to be tough, unapproachable, stressed, burdened, and often socially awkward. Blame it on the burden of leadership or the fact that it can be lonely at the top (often because of all the bridges burnt along the journey). but being a leader means that people are following you, and who wants to follow that?! People want to feel safe and inspired under a leader but not fearful. We want to feel a connection to our leader and know where we are going.

The reason joy isn't often associated with leadership is because there is a huge misconception that joy isn't strong. I blame history. History has recorded countless accounts about leaders who were brave, ruthless, long-suffering, selfless, powerful, peaceful, talented, and even funny (but those stories usually end in tragedy). Where are the accounts of the exceptionally joyful?

Jesus was a joyful leader. He was on mission, but still attentive and available to those around him. He wasn't afraid to stop what he was doing to attend to a need or enjoy a special moment. Jesus was all about teamwork. He prioritized people's development over perfection. He invited and made room for all manner of people to join his team if they were willing to go where he was going. Everywhere he went he left a wake of goodness and glory. He did all of this while literally carrying the weight of the future of the world on his shoulders!

The burden of leadership

As a leader in your home, classroom, the office, on the field, or in the community, you are responsible for many things. Depending on your role you may be responsible for making life or death decisions, ensuring others safety, providing gainful employment for individuals who provide for their families, or shaping the minds and hearts of people entrusted to you. That's a lot of pressure for someone who also needs to lead their own life.

The "burden of leadership" is real, and it should be, because it's serious business, but it doesn't mean we must be crushed by it. Too often, leaders are burnt out because they are too busy taking care of everyone else that they forget to care for themselves. They've been hurt, betrayed, made mistakes that had a great effect on many, and they don't often trust people. But the good news is that leaders are not disqualified from the good news!

Jesus invites all of us to hand him our burdens and He will bear them. In return for trusting the Lord, he gives us strategy, energy, focus, and rest. Please don't misunderstand, I realize this isn't as easy as it sounds. Culturally, we are conditioned to want to be the hero, the only one who can save the day. There is something deep within that even likes to be the martyr and suffer for the cause. The "I can do it on my own" mentality is not from the Lord. That kind of thinking comes from the enemy who wants us to be isolated, burdened, and constantly crushed under pressure. This does not mean that there wont be times when we are called to go alone, or lead way out in front, but like Moses who was overwhelmed by his assignment to lead the Israelites, we can receive this same promise from the Lord, "My Presence will go with you, and I will give you rest" (Exodus 33:14 NIV).

Yes, the burden of leadership is heavy, but Jesus is offering the great yoke exchange. We don't have to be crushed by its weight. We don't have to fake it and pretend to be something we aren't—untouchable or superhuman. We can boast about our weakness because he is strong!

Done be strong, be joyful

It's a battle out there! Only the strong survive, at least according to evolutionary theory. We'll try anything to increase our strength (or the perception of our strength): energy drinks, workout routines, meditation, expensive clothing, higher education, vitamin supplements, and whatever the latest fad may be. If it increases stamina, power, strength, focus, elasticity (looking at you Collagen), and energy, we want it. Billions of dollars are spent each year in the pursuit of enhancement. Clearly, we are desperate for more strength.

Historically, leaders couldn't ever appear weak, or their enemies would attempt a takeover. Therefore, they would go to extreme lengths to appear strong. Rulers would make gargantuan statues of themselves, build massive walls around their cities, and establish great fear in the hearts of their servants and subjects by enacting heinous acts of violence on a whim. These leadership tactics are still in place, albeit a bit more subtle.

We are not a surprise to the Lord. He knows that leading requires great strength, that's why he is always extending the invitation to draw on his power and might, but unfortunately most often we ignore it. Instead, we never lose that little toddler voice inside that says, "Me do it!" We want to be like the tough guys, the great ones. We believe the lie that to be a hero we have to do it on our own. But let's look at the real heroes.

The heroes in scripture (Abraham, Moses, Joseph, Paul, Jesus, and many others), did amazing things, but they didn't do it in their own power and strength. Paul states many times that it was God's strength he relied on. Joseph and Daniel both credit their dream interpretation to the power of God working through them. Solomon, the wisest person to ever live, was given wisdom from heaven. Moses told the Lord he wasn't going anywhere unless God went before him. Jesus had every reason to boast about his power and strength, but he wasn't motivated by people idolizing him. His greatest desire was to glorify his Father. Each of these are examples of people placing their faith and confidence in the Lord, relying on his strength to accomplish more than they could ask, think, or imagine.

It's not a cop out. God's not trying to sit you on the sidelines or minimize your contribution, quite the contrary! He wants to *use* you to accomplish wonderful things and he wants to do it in a way that doesn't destroy you, your family, or those around you. Drawing from the unending well of God's resources is how we can be our best for the long haul. That is what God wants for us. Zachariah 4:6 (NIV) reads, "Not by might, nor by power, but by my Spirit says the Lord Almighty." God has given us a gift and we do well to accept it.

What we've come to know is that God doesn't do anything without joy. If we are going to lead powered by the Spirit of God, then joy is going to be included in our leadership. Bill Johnson says, "Our strength is actually measured by our measure of joy." You want to be a strong leader? Nehemiah 8:10 reminds us that our strength comes from the joy we have in the Lord. It's counterintuitive, I know. Instead of spending so much time, money, and effort to build strength (or the appearance of strength) on our own, all we need to do is accept the Lord's offer. The more our joy in the Lord grows, the stronger we become. I like to say, "Don't be strong, be joyful!"

It's incredible. The fact that the Lord gives us so much access to his presence, love, and power even when we have a history of misusing it. We struggle to trust him, and yet he trusts us.

It's personal

Headlines are filled with stories of leaders getting caught and kicked out. We are shocked and full of disdain when we read and hear about abuse, affairs, stealing, lying, and a whole lot of dark secrets. Why are there so many leaders doing terrible things and leaving damage and destruction in their wake? Unfortunately, this isn't anything new, it's just more public. At the speed at which information travels, we are much more aware of stories across the globe, and because bad news sells, news travels fast.

The problem of failed leadership isn't only found in the business, church, or government sectors. It can't be blamed on a lack of education or easily pinned on the mess that was already there. The poor leadership of others begins with poor leadership of self. The sneaky embezzlement, the secret affair, the abuse of employees, the extreme greed, and the intentional covering up of problems are not just issues that suddenly manifest when there is a title and corner office. They begin in the heart.

The best way to become a good leader is to lead yourself well (which is why we started with that in this section). This doesn't mean that you will automatically be an ingenious entrepreneur or a high-powered executive, but it means you can be trusted. When the foundation is solid, the building will stand. When the foundation is broken, it will eventually crumble. Sounds biblical, doesn't it? And here's another one, what is inside will eventually come out. Jesus knew what he was talking about. As the pressure of life bears down on us, what's really inside will be revealed. The Joy Bringer journey has intentionally led us through the areas of healing and forgiveness so that we can love and lead others with joy.

The truth is that a leader is held to a higher account because they are entrusted with God's priceless treasure, not ideas or things, but people.

ICNU

Often as leaders of others (in the home and in the workplace) we are convinced that if we don't show up or do it ourselves it won't get done. We believe that if we take a break then others will think we are lazy, or the world will stop spinning. There are times when this may be true (babies need to be fed, your book can only be written by you, the idea in your head can only come out of you, etc.), but most of the time there is an opportunity to empower others to step up and learn. Odds are, someone gave you a chance, and while there was a learning curve (there always is), it helped you get to where you are now. The Lord intends to use you to do his work, and part of that work is to raise up others.

Jesus models this in such a powerful way. His disciples were a bunch of knuckleheads. They fought with each other, were slow to grasp the things he was teaching, and they denied and betrayed him. Yet, Jesus still gave them power and authority. He saw their potential. He called it out in them and had grace and patience to walk alongside them as they grew.

It's a risk to give authority and responsibility to someone young or inexperienced. It's a risk to set your pride aside and encourage someone to grow beyond your capacity. It's a risk to imagine raising up your replacement. But through healing and faith it is possible. People aren't threats; they are gifts. Even those who have ulterior motives can be included at the table. Jesus knew from the beginning that Judas would betray him and yet he gave him a chance to be a part of the team and learn. God cares about what and who he's entrusted to you. We don't want our insecurity to get in the way of the amazing things he can accomplish.

ICNU is a great tool to help you identify and encourage those the Lord brings your way. It simply stands for, I See In You. It's a great way to communicate to those around you that you believe in their potential. Here are some examples:

- I see in you a real ability with numbers.
- I see in you a gift of working with children.
- I see in you a knack with problem solving.
- I see in you a joyful leader.

As a leader it's an honor and privilege to have someone follow you. What are you going to do with their time and attention? Encourage and teach, lead them to new heights and share with them the joy you know. It can be a daunting task, but the Joy Bringer's core values are intended to give you handles to hold so you can maintain your joy and bring it everywhere you go. Remember this:

- When bitterness and burden bear down, grab a hold of **GRATITUDE**. Being **grateful** for the opportunity to lead and the gift of the ever-present Helper.
- When people hurt you and betray your trust, grab hold of **FORGIVENESS**. Actively **forgiving** those who hurt and betray you helps keep love as the highest goal and encourages joy to continually fill your heart.
- Not if, but when things change, find your footing by grabbing onto **FLEXIBILITY**. Staying **flexible** and open to

the voice of the Spirit not just through intentional time spent with the Lord, but through others at all levels who speak with wisdom and valued experience.

- Instead of burning out from stress and striving, grab hold of **REST** (the last Joy Bringer's Core Value). Choosing to prioritize **rest** as an act of worship, confirming your identity as a child of God and being refreshed from the well of his goodness will help you lead from joy.

Dear reader, whether you are a student, a parent, a CEO, a laborer, or all of the above and everything in between, you have been gifted. You are positioned to influence those around you and lead them with love and joy to Jesus. You are a leader! Your personality, temperament, and unique characteristics are what make you special. The Lord wants you to stand strong in your calling and joyfully lead.

JOY BRINGER CHALLENGE

I challenge you to begin to use ICNU with people around you.

Chapter 18:

Not All Joy

Who doesn't cry like a baby while watching *Steel Magnolias*? I played Annelle in the stage version of this movie (the Daryl Hannah role). Fun fact: *Steel Magnolias* was a play before it was a movie, and it lands in the top ten of my favorite on stage experiences. One of the many famous lines from the movie is, "Laughter through tears is my favorite emotion." Another fun fact: that line is not in the play. An acting professor in college posed this question to our class, "On a scale of one to ten, which emotion ranks the highest?" Most people guessed anger or crying, but no one got it right. He said, "None. It's a trick question. All emotions are a seven." He meant that no emotion or expression of emotion is more important or more powerful than another. They also aren't exclusive; we commonly experience multiple emotions at once.

Often, people assume that if you are a joyful person, then you must not have struggles or pain. Many assume that I have it easy, therefore I can preach about joy. On the contrary! I am qualified to speak on joy because I've been through pain, suffering, loss, trauma, depression, anxiety, and fear and can attest that joy found in Jesus outlasts all those things. We know by now that joy isn't happiness or based on our circumstance or mood. That's why the Joy Bringer's Core Values are so important to me. They are tried and tested! I use them every day (even when I don't want to).

Joy is present tense

"What time is it?" I asked regularly. "Time to get a watch" my mom would reply like clockwork (pun intended). Despite the many watches she would buy me, I didn't like wearing them. I also didn't like alarm clocks. I had one, but I preferred my mom to wake me up. Her loud and enthusiastic renditions of "Wake up little Season" (her spin on the song "Wake up little Susie" by the Everly Brothers), "Rise and Shine" (a Sunday School classic), or "Good Morning" (from *Singin' in the Rain*) were much better than the jarring and unfriendly clammer of the dreaded alarm clock. Plus, it was always entertaining to see how she would fit my name into the songs.

My name, Season, means "appointed time." Like many, I struggle to be in the moment. I am always looking ahead, anticipating what's next and thinking, "Is it time? How about now? What's going to happen? What if it doesn't work out?" I have said things like, "Things will be better when…" or "I just need to get through these few weeks and then life will be easier." The reality is, joy, ease, peace, or success don't live in the future. That's where anxiety lives, in the unknown.

"Those were the good ol' days." Do you know someone who is obsessed with the past? I do! They say things like, "I miss the way things used to be." Maybe that's you. Always reminiscing about the times "back in the day" when life was good, when you were at your best or things were just how you wanted them. It can be easy to get stuck in the past. We either miss the good times and long for what was, or we are burdened under the weight of our past pain. Depression thrives in our fixation on or the bondage of our past.

The A Word

Acceptance is a word I used to hate. I believed acceptance implied one was settling, complacent, and accepting defeat. It was my therapist who helped redefine this word for me. I was traumatized and deeply depressed from a recent string of loss and tragedy in my life and terrified of what could be around the corner. I was completely fixated on the worst-case scenario and riddled with anxiety. There I was, helpless, paralyzed, and ashamed. I felt like a hypocrite. How could I preach joy in every circumstance when I could barely get out of bed? That's when Max, our ninja therapist, dropped the A word. Acceptance. He helped me understand the importance of allowing myself to be present in the moment, the here and now. I couldn't change what happened in the past, and I couldn't control the future. At that particular moment I was safe. I had what I needed. I was aware that Jesus was with me. That's where joy is found. Joy is present tense.

There will be times when we find ourselves walking through the valley of the shadow of death (Psalm 23:4). When we do, it's important to recognize a few things. First, we are being led by the Good Shepherd. He never leads us and leaves. Jesus is always there, protecting us, leading us *through it*. Second, the valley is where we find rest. There is no climbing, only meadows and streams of refreshment. Third, the shadows are just that, illusions. Shadows only appear when there is a light source, and the light that is with you is Jesus. Fourth, the valley is where beautiful things grow. If you've ever climbed a high mountain, you'll know that once you hit a certain elevation, there are no more trees or flowers, mostly just sand, rocks or shrubs. The beautiful things don't grow up high. When we are up on the mountain, beauty is found by looking back down.

Joy doesn't live in the future. Joy doesn't live in the past. Awareness and acceptance of where we are gives us a chance to assess what we have and what we need. Joy is found in the present.

Incredible inflatable joy

Remember the movie, *The Incredibles*? Mr. and Mrs. Incredible hung up their superhero capes and masks for parenthood, but they end up fighting for justice and peace with their whole family in matching super gear. Each member of the family had a unique superpower (strength, invisibility, and speed). Mom's superpower was flexibility (hmm, interesting! Sounds like a Joy Bringer's Core Value at work). They called her "Elastigirl." In the end she finds herself in a position to save her children as they are about to be bombed out of the sky. She stretches around them to create a protective shield and as they plummet toward the ocean she stretches into a parachute. They survive the attack but are stranded, dogpaddling in the middle of the ocean with no help in sight and land far off in the distance. Invisigirl (her daughter) says, "Do you expect us to *swim* there?!" Her Mom replies, "I expect you to trust me." On cue, Elastigirl turns into a boat that sails them safely to shore.

Joy is buoyant, it floats. Our trust in Jesus, the one who is ever present and always faithful, keeps us from sinking into an ocean of despair and hopelessness. That doesn't mean we always *feel* joyful, but the presence of Jesus in our deepest pain and trial means that we have access to strength and joy. We are not disqualified from the good stuff even when we are in the middle of the difficulty. Jesus is our peace. He is our protection. He is our firm foundation. Like Elastigirl, Jesus provides a safe vessel for us to be in, even when the ocean around us is dark, the waves are high, and the current is strong.

I will never forget the phone call late in the evening. A friend and fellow pastor called to say that our friend Adriana's husband had been in a surfing accident. He was found on the shore and taken to the hospital. Adriana was being driven to the hospital and we rallied the pastoral team, piled in a few cars, and descended on the emergency room. There were prayer warriors stomping the halls of that hospital, laying hands on him, and bringing her soda and tissues. At some point, her five children were brought to the hospital as well and instructed to say goodbye. It was brutal but beautiful.

At the end of the worst day of their lives, her five children were asleep in their beds, and she was alone. As her mind was trying to process what had just happened, she realized she didn't know how to be a widow, so she Googled it. "How to be a widow?" The first thing that came up was a blog from a woman who was using casual sex as a way to heal from her loss. That wasn't what she was looking for. She asked the Lord, "Who am I going to be now?" "The Best Widow Ever" he said. And she is.

Adriana grieved. We grieved with her. She also held onto Jesus, her joy. She laughed, cried, secretly played a generosity game, and anonymously gave away as much as she could, and did her best to survive. In fact, that was her goal: to stay alive. While there was extreme pain in each day, she also found immense joy. She discovered that she could indeed use power tools, and that Jesus was closer than she ever knew. She didn't have to choose between joy and sorrow. Jesus was there amid the pain. She was living Psalm

30:5 (NKJV), which says, "Weeping may endure for a night, but joy comes in the morning." The light of love and the joy of Jesus shone into the darkness. With each sunrise, her tragedy lost its sting and joy rewrote her story for the glory of God.

Garden therapy

"How much more can I take, Jesus?!" Wave after wave of tragedy and pain kept rolling over me. At some point it became almost comical—almost. I was in my backyard watering, pulling weeds, and singing to my plants through sobs, snot, and tears. I had never planted a garden and the 2020 pandemic life seemed like the perfect opportunity. I was home and had time to spare. It felt good to take my focus off my sorrows and the mountain of things beyond my control and try to cultivate life. My daily gardening time became my time of prayer and worship. I am sure my neighbors were very well acquainted with the state of my life because they probably heard all about it through the fence.

The Lord taught me so much about his love and care for me as I tended my own garden. I felt buried, just like the seeds in the ground. While I was experiencing what felt like a dark and painful death, the Lord was caring for the soil, watering, and shining his bright love on me, even when I couldn't see it or feel it. Underground in the dark I was breaking open to sprout roots, growing and stretching, pushing up through the dirt, desperate for light and air. The Lord was near, singing and speaking words of life and encouragement over me just as I did with my plants. As my weak and tiny self was doing my best to survive in the new unknown environment, God was protecting me from the annoying lizards that wanted to feast on my weakness and ruin my progress (the gang of backyard lizards were my nemesis). When I began to grow stronger and taller, sprouting leaves, the Lord was cheering me on, proud of each little bud. The labor of growth was finally beginning to bear fruit and I knew the Lord was still there. My needs changed but God knew exactly what I needed.

The Lord knows our fears, pain, and deepest longings. Scripture says that our tears are precious to him (Psalm 56:8). Not only does he cherish them, but they are also not wasted. Our tears are a beautiful part of the process. They help enrich the soil. They add flavor, texture, and sweetness to our joy. Psalm 126:5 says, "Those who plant in tears will harvest with shouts of joy." This is a promise. When there are tears, there will be joy.

Not all joy

Seasons of darkness, pain and trial can feel relentless, unending, and all-consuming. It's neither kind nor accurate to tell someone who is suffering to, "Consider it all joy!" James, the author of this phrase in the New Testament that is way too often quoted at someone in the depths of despair, never intended for his words to be insensitive or cruel (James 1:2). He's encouraging his readers to be sure to see the bigger picture. He wants them to keep their eyes open to the truth that the Lord will use the trials and difficulties to strengthen them and to reveal his glory. The enemy's attack is a reminder to keep our eyes locked on the goodness, faithfulness, and power of God. We are to remember the promise of God and find our strength in him.

It sounds simple, but when you're caught in a spiral being sucked deeper into depression and anxiety, it can seem almost impossible. I found myself in one of those moments. After a string of intense trauma and massive change, I found myself alone, sitting in silence and calm for the first time in months. It was there that my adrenaline stopped raging and I began to feel the impact of what we had just experienced. Instead of welcoming the peace, I was pulled down deep, drowning in the emotions I hadn't had a chance to feel. For weeks, I could not stop crying. Even though things seemed settled, I was terrified they would change at any moment.

Sitting in a fog of silence and pain, I scrolled through social media and found a quote from Lysa TerKeurst. She said, "You steer where you stare." It shook me awake. I realized I had locked eyes with the worst-case scenario and every moment felt like I was speeding toward it. For the first time in months, I blinked. My eyes struggled to refocus but as I looked around, I saw Jesus. His loving eyes, the smile, his hand extended and the peaceful confidence that assured me, "Just look at me. I will lead you, protect you, and show you my goodness." Locking eyes with Jesus, my source of hope, my joy, I knew I could grieve in safety.

I want to be clear, it's not all joy. There are things that are ugly, painful, dark, and scary. There is an enemy and he is up to no good. But we have a savior who is victorious over all things and leaves every situation stamped, "very good." We may not see it right away—or at all, until we have a heavenly perspective—but, like I always say, "God will get his!" He will get the win. He will get his glory and that is where we find joy.

We are not promised ease. Scripture never claims that our faith will keep us from attack, the fire, the storm nor the loss. What we are promised is that the Lord will never leave us nor forsake us (Hebrews 13:5). In fact, Scripture reminds us that "The Lord is near to the brokenhearted" (Psalm 34:18 ESV). The love, compassion, power, and protection of God is with us through it all. It's not all going to be joy, but the Joy Bringer will be in all.

JOY BRINGER CHALLENGE

I challenge you to spend the day being in the moment. Be in today. This is harder than you think. We are conditioned to think and plan ahead so we rarely are aware of the current moment. Joy is present tense, remember? So, I encourage you today to be in joy. As you eat, be aware of the texture, color, feel, and taste of each bite. As you drive, take in your surroundings, discover something new that you've never noticed before. At home, identify your favorite room or corner and be aware of why you enjoy it. Find joy in your tasks or work today. Appreciate the process and your ability to do the work. Jesus is in every moment. I challenge you to look for him and lock eyes with joy.

Chapter 19:

Joy Bringer

Joy verse

"And then he told them, 'Go into all the world and preach the
Good News to everyone.'"—Mark 16:15 NLT

Billboards can be a great marketing tool. I was on one for about
a year. My face was an advertisement for a long-running 80's
musical in San Diego. People would stop me and ask if that was
my face on Interstate 8. I would say, "Yes! Come see *Mixtape!*"
There are many ways to catch people's eye. Driving across the
country you'll see varied attempts to inform, attract, and capture
people's attention. The goal is action. The billboards I don't find
very enticing are the ones that try to scare people into believing
in Jesus. Because nothing says, "good news" and "love" like fear
and Old English, right?

The word "evangelism" has a mixed reputation. The tactics
vary, from strangers shoving outdated Bible tracts in your face on
the sidewalk and people with bullhorns shouting, "turn or burn,"
to brave missionaries journeying to unreached people groups, and
powerful preachers leading millions of people to Jesus. Most of

us fall somewhere in the middle and don't quite know what to do with the Great Commission that tells us to go out into the world and preach the gospel. We might have many concerns and questions, such as, "Where should I go? What would I say? What if I am rejected? I'm not an expert in the Christian faith, how could I answer anyone's questions? I don't know how to convert anyone!" Relax! That's not exactly what the Lord is asking you to do.

Being a Joy Bringer is an everyday lifestyle. We are people changed by the love of Jesus and live like it. We are natural walking, talking carriers of the good news. Whether you are a loudmouth or not, your life shines, and others are watching. Let's lead them to Jesus.

Thermostat vs. thermometer

Like many couples, my husband and I don't agree on the ideal temperature of our bedroom. He likes it to be cold at night with the fan on, but warm under the covers. I, on the other hand, would prefer not to sleep in the arctic tundra. I bundle up with blankets covering my body and a pillow on my head. I also cover parts of my face because my nose gets frostbite. My husband complains that he's still hot but then he touches me with his feet that feel cold as ice. While I don't appreciate it now, I'm sure someday when the dreaded hot flashes take effect, I will be grateful for his frosty toes.

During the pandemic, we all became familiar with temperature checks. Having our foreheads scanned to get a thermal reading was a regular occurrence to be granted entrance into restaurants, stores, or other gatherings. There isn't too much of a difference between our individual temperatures (unless you're sick). But have you noticed that one person can really change the "temperature" of a room?

You've probably heard stories of the oddball method actors who wreak havoc on a movie set. Not every actor demands to be only referred to by their character name, but actors are often dramatic people. They are trained to share their emotions in order to impact a room. They are conduits, choosing to go on an emotional journey for the sake of the audience's experience. Being in a room full of actors can be overwhelming. Imagine doing it day in and day out for months at a time. To help maintain our sanity, would often place a sign on the greenroom or dressing room door that said, "Please be responsible for the energy you bring into this room."

You may not always know when it happens, you could be perfectly fine and then someone enters a room carrying the weight of the world on their shoulders and you suddenly feel it too. Or if there is tension between people you may find yourself swept into the current of anger and frustration. Being a thermometer means you are at the mercy of the environment, affected by your surroundings.

You are a powerful person. You carry the goodness, love, peace, and joy of the Lord inside of you. When you walk into a room you bring joy and Jesus! Instead of being emotionally tossed or assaulted by the energy of others, you can be a thermostat! You have the power to change and set the temperature of a room. By being attentive to the Spirit and asking the right questions, you will know how the Lord wants to use you to impact a room.

It begins by being aware of our internal temperatures. When we know where we stand, we can increase our sensitivity to the atmosphere of the room. Asking the Lord to give you eyes to see and ears to hear will help you understand what is going on in a room and how he wants you to contribute. This doesn't mean that you become a clown doing tricks to make the group laugh, or a fixer trying to make everyone get along. It means you are available to pray in the spirit for heaviness to be lifted, or to share a perspective of hope. If there is gossip and slander happening, you get to change the subject or offer truth. Being a thermostat means *you* get to set the temperature of the room.

Location, location, location

I love to travel. Whether it's to speak at an event, or exploring the world with my husband, I can't get enough of new people and places. For me, it's easy to become enamored by everywhere else and overlook the beauty and opportunity in my hometown. For years we lived in a place that I considered to be temporary. We knew that it was only for a season, and I struggled to find deep meaning or connection.

"You can't have authority over that which you do not love." My friend Christina (the one with the core values list) said this and it struck down deep. I wanted to be effective in the world. I had big dreams, and they all began "out there." I had closed off my heart to the people and community where I was planted. I began to realize the Lord wasn't waiting for me to be at a certain location at a certain time in the future to use me. He had placed great power and ability inside me, and I wasn't tapping into it because I thought I needed to be "on mission" to the ends of the earth. That's when I fell in love.

The Lord loves your community and your neighbors. He wants to reach them as much as he longs to reveal his goodness and love to those in the next city over, the other side of the country, and the most remote places in the world. We must tune our hearts to the frequency of love God has for our specific location. That's where our mission begins. You may be called to bring the good news to the ends of the earth, but it starts where you are right now.

It feels safer to wait for "someday." It's easier to love people from afar than to get in the trenches and risk getting dirty. I've often heard people say, "I'm called to the people of Africa (or another far-off place)." I often reply, "Great! Praise the Lord." And follow up with, "How are you loving the people in your neighborhood right now?" We get blinded by the big calling and become satisfied with just the dream. But the dream won't become a reality if we fail to do the work needed in the here and now. Scripture is clear that if we are faithful in the little things then we can be trusted with more (Luke 16:10).

Where you are right this very minute is exactly the place God wants to use you. Open your heart to love the people in your community. We moved from Southern California to Tennessee. Before we landed in Knoxville (a city that seemed more like home), we lived in a small rural town. I might as well have moved to another planet! At first, I felt so displaced and even confused. I asked, "What are we doing here?!" But here's the truth, I have fallen in love with Hillbillies (their label, not mine)! My new neighbors would laugh at me. We were so different! They didn't understand my love for vegetables and salad or my fitness habits, but they knew how much I loved them. I've had the privilege to walk with them through life while sitting with them on the front porch. And they have done so much for me. By opening my heart to people I knew nothing about and who I never imagined associating with, I have been so blessed and, dare I even say, changed.

The power of story

Author and speaker, Patti Digh says, "The shortest distance between two people is a story." Have you ever heard someone's story and said, "Me too!"? Our common human experience is meant to cross borders and unite us. We all have pain, loss, love, hopes, dreams, and scars. The thing that helped me get out of bed the morning after my mother died was the idea that everyone on this planet will experience the death of a loved one. I was not alone in my experience of grief. When I meet someone who has loved someone else's children, is an only child and lost both of their parents, or who also has a deep love for wiener dogs, we immediately have a greater understanding of each other and a common bond.

Even when others don't share our exact experience, we all have the same set of needs. We need to be loved, have certainty/security, feel significant, contribute, and have the opportunity to grow. When we find something that helps meet these needs, we share the goods. That's why advertising campaigns are filled with slogans like, "It worked for me!"

Do it again

You don't need to be a biblical scholar, fancy preacher, or exotic missionary to preach the gospel. The gospel of Jesus is the good news of his love, power, freedom, and presence in your life. Of course, there is always the opportunity to learn more. Knowing and understanding the Bible is wise and beneficial, but the people we read about in the New Testament who were radically changed by Jesus weren't experts in the Hebrew Scriptures! They ran off to tell anyone who would listen about their encounter with Jesus. Let's look at a few examples of this from the Bible.

Example One: The woman at the well had a life-changing encounter with Jesus that compelled her to tell others. When she said, "Come and see a man who told me everything I ever did!" (John 4:29), people wanted to meet Jesus and experience him for themselves (John 4:30). So they came in droves. It was the power of her story that sent the entire village running to meet him.

Example Two: The entire community knew him as the blind beggar, but once he encountered Jesus, his identity was forever changed. His story, "I was blind but now I see" was all it took for people to believe that the power of Jesus was real. Both the religious elite and the common folk went in search of Jesus to find out more (John 9).

Example Three: After seeing him killed, buried, and now alive, Mary had a mission. She couldn't stop until they all knew the good news. Jesus was alive (John 20)!

Your story, or testimony, of how you have been changed by the love of Jesus carries more power than you can imagine. The root meaning of the Hebrew word for testimony means, "Do it again." When you share what God has done for you with others, you are declaring, "He did it for me, and he can do it for you!"

People can get freaked out at the thought of sharing their testimony. It can be very vulnerable, and we often don't know where to start. Our stories are complex and have taken our lifetime to develop. They can also be dramatic and full of gory details. A good storyteller knows that it's important to understand your audience. If your story contains explicit details that aren't appropriate for all audiences, it's okay to have a broader version that gets the point across without gory specifics. But then again, there are some people who need to hear *all* the details and you have the freedom to share.

Just like it's important to know your audience, it's important to be ready with a clear and concise story. 1 Peter 3:15 says, "Always be prepared to give an answer to everyone who asks you to give the reason for the hope that you have. But do this with gentleness and respect." This is where the two-minute testimony becomes your new friend.

Every story has a beginning, a middle, and an end. The two-minute testimony is a simple way to help us break down our stories so that they are clear and easily shared. It is one of the best tools in a Joy Bringer's belt. This three-question prompt will help you create your own. I've included some examples that may help.

Two-minute testimony

What was your life like before you met Jesus?

Simply share the things you felt and any major events that led up to that point. Here are a few examples:

- "I was lost, broken, and searching for something to make me feel like I mattered. I got caught up in drugs and after years of abuse, I hit rock bottom..."
- "I was born and raised in the church, but I was disillusioned by the drama and fake people, and I walked away from my faith when I entered college. I got married and had a few kids and one day my youngest child got very sick..."

When/How did you encounter the Lord?

Sometimes it's all of a sudden, other times it's a gradual awareness, but when we encounter the presence and love of Jesus it changes us. Here are a few examples:

- "I was sitting on my bed writing my suicide note, when suddenly I heard a voice that said, 'Do you know I love you?' I was so overcome with peace and love that I never felt before. I knew it was Jesus."
- "I didn't know where else to turn so I got in my car and found myself in the parking lot of a church in my community. After many minutes of debate, I got up the nerve to go in. I didn't know anyone, but it felt like the preacher was preaching right to me! When he asked if anyone

wanted to say "yes" to the love of Jesus, my hand shot up over my head."

What is your life like now?

Even though your life isn't over, the "ending" of your testimony is where you are now. What's changed since you met Jesus? It may sound something like this:

- "I don't know how to explain it, but since accepting Jesus into my life, everything is different! I have hope for the first time and I know I am not alone."
- "The power of Jesus is real. He healed me and I will never be the same."
- "I still face challenges in my life each day. But now that I have Jesus, I know that I am not alone. I have strength and joy and a community that loves me."

Your story is your own. It's beautiful, powerful, a celebration of God's goodness and glory, and it is meant to be shared. It will bring joy to those around you and your good news will be their good news!

JOY BRINGER CHALLENGE

I challenge you to think through and write out your two-minute testimony and share it with someone this week!

1. What was your life like before you met Jesus?

_____

_____

_____

_____

_____

_____

_____

_____

_____

_____

2. When/how did you encounter the Lord?

_____

_____

_____

_____

_____

_____

_____

3. What is your life like now?

_____

_____

_____

_____

_____

_____

_____

Chapter 20:

Joy Bringer's Core Value—Rest

Joy verse

"Let the faithful rejoice that he honors them. Let them sing for joy as they lie on their beds."–Psalm 149:5 NLT

There was a rule in the theatre where I spent most of my career called, "the bloody stump rule." While unwritten and (mostly) unspoken, this decree dictated our lives. You've probably heard the phrase, "The show must go on." Well, that's what this rule was all about. You went onstage even if you had lost a limb and were left with a bloody stump. Born and raised in the theatre, I was accustomed to the reality that no matter what, you never miss a performance. This meant I didn't attend weddings, funerals, baby showers, family vacations, or anything that was scheduled in the afternoons, evenings, or weekends. The only way to get theatre people to attend something is if it's very late at night (after 11 p.m.) or on a Monday (the one day most actors have off).

Most of my life I've taken pride in and boasted in my exemplary commitment and work ethic. I married my first husband on a Monday and was back on stage the next day. I buried my mother in the morning, went to a rehearsal in the afternoon, and performed in a different show that evening. Sacrificing for the art was what I (and most actors) do. I valued my reputation for loyalty and commitment over my health and wellbeing. My identity was wrapped up in my profession. It was my whole life, and I wore it like a badge. I was an actor with a capital "A."

I came to realize that my so called "work ethic" wasn't a good thing, it was deeply rooted in pride, worthlessness and desperation. My pride said, "I will be the first one to arrive and the last one to leave. I don't take a day off because I am superhuman, above those weak ones who need things like that." But really, I was speaking from a place of fear and worthlessness saying, "I need to prove that I am valuable. If I work harder, I will be loved more." I was desperate to feel secure and valued.

As a culture, we have been so conditioned to believe that hard work and commitment means forsaking all else. We are told that working forty hours a week isn't enough to achieve success because the real competitors log sixty to eighty hours a week or more. "I'll rest when I'm dead" is something I've heard more times than I can count, as if rest is for the weak and unsuccessful. We make fun of and ridicule high profile people who have mental breakdowns in public, but still expect superhuman production and total accessibility. Time off in this country is a luxury while the leading cause for medical leave and disability is mental health issues.

Having boundaries and choosing rest and health is not rewarded in our culture. No one is celebrated for their choices to work the agreed upon hours and take all their vacation. When was the last time you were promoted or given a raise for choosing your well-being over the deadline? Thankfully, there is a long overdue movement toward work-life balance, mental health care, and rest. The pandemic brought about some good in forcing us to slow down and adjust our "normal" rhythm of life. But unlearning a lifetime of cultural and personal expectations and habits isn't easy.

Jesus not only led a perfect life (without sin), but he is also touted as being the best leader ever to have walked the face of the earth. He is also famous for resting. Not just any resting! Jesus napped in the middle of storms. He took time away when there was a never-ending line of people vying for his attention. He rested with friends, and he rested alone. For Jesus, rest was not about religion; it was about life. Rest was a core value for Jesus, and it is the fourth Joy Bringer's Core Value.

Holy defiance

The hardest thing for me about resting is shutting off the "shoulds" in my head. I think about all the things I have to accomplish in order to meet the standards of not only myself, but of those around me. But leading (myself and others) from a place of joy is only possible when I am filled with it.

In the creation story found in Genesis, chapters one and two, we see that God blesses three things, the animals, humans, and the day of rest (Genesis 1:22, 28, 2:2). God has given us the blessing of time. How many times have you wished that you had more hours in a day or could stop time? Well, the Lord has done that for us! He has declared the day of rest as holy, meaning set apart.

Not long after the Israelites were freed from centuries of slavery in Egypt, the Lord gave them the Ten Commandments. I can only imagine that the fourth commandment was especially exciting for them. "Remember the Sabbath day and keep it holy." In other words, a day off for all! The full version exclusively states that everyone, including women, children, servants, and animals will rest on that day. Why? Because God rested. This is a big deal. The Lord was identifying not just the Israelites, but even servants (who were often not Hebrew) as his own. God was affirming people as his beloved children—children of God, not slaves to the King (Exodus 20:8-11).

As slaves under Pharaoh, the Israelites *never* had a day off. They labored seven days a week under a ruthless ruler who considered himself a god. Now the one true Lord, God Almighty, was comparing the people to himself. Essentially, God was saying, "If I rested on the seventh day, you can too." Woah! That had to be crazy! So each week, the Sabbath was a celebration of their identity as children of God, not slaves. Their rest was an act of worship unto their good Father in heaven. Rest honored God as their provider, placing their trust in him to do his good work.

Rest is vital to maintain joy as we lead our own lives and as leaders of others. When we make rest a core value, we are practicing holy defiance. Rest is an act of rebellion against the enemy who taunts us with the questions, "Are you sure? Are you sure you have enough? Are you sure you are worthy? Are you sure you are loved?" When we rest, we say no to the pressure and demands of the never satisfied world, and yes to the invitation to trust our faithful and powerful God who unconditionally loves us. Resting in the truth of who God is and who he says we are helps refuel us and fill us with joy so we can bring it everywhere we go.

A gift, not a curse

We place a lot of blame on Adam and Eve. It's often thought that because of their big screw up we have been cursed with labor. But that's not true. Work was a blessing, a gift from the Lord in the garden before the fall. Adam was given the opportunity to name the animals and that was no small job! Before the fall, Adam and Eve were given the charge to care and cultivate, to govern and create (Genesis 1:28-30).

In Hebraic culture, it was expected that the first-born son would do what his father did. If the father was a farmer, the son would be too. Jesus was a carpenter (or more accurately, stone mason), like his earthly father, Joseph (Matthew 13:55, Mark 6:3). But Jesus also did what his heavenly Father did. Jesus said, "My Father is always working, and so am I" (John 5:17). He also said, "I tell you the truth, the Son can do nothing by himself. He does only what he sees the Father doing. Whatever the Father does, the Son also does" (John 5:19). We are created in the image of God. And just as God worked, each of us is given the opportunity to participate. We have been given talents and gifts to impact the world around us. The work of our hands, hearts, and minds reflects our Father. Work is a beautiful gift!

The enemy loves to take the good gifts of the Father and twist them into a burden. If he can get us to believe that we are, in fact, not children of God but slaves, we see work as a curse and not a gift. When we believe the lie that we are worthless then we turn to striving, trying to earn approval and favor. For me, this desire to earn approval from God and man has led me to exhaustion and extreme burnout more than once.

As sons and daughters of the Most High King, we are not asked to produce, we get to participate in the divinity of creation! Let that sink in. Just like our Creator God and Father, we get to create and rest. It's what sets us apart. Slaves work out of fear and strive to please their master. Children create and rest in joy, and their Father is delighted by both.

If you are anything like me, you may be already planning on how you are going to rest really well. I think, "OK, if I am commanded to rest, I am going to rest so hard, I'll be the best at it!" and once again I fall into the trap of performance and striving. So how do we know when it's rest? When it feels like an invitation.

The Lord knows the temptation we face to strive and the pressure to perform. His "command" is to, "Remember the Sabbath." Hear it as an invitation, a loving reminder to follow him. Read these words of Jesus from Matthew 11:28-30 (MSG) out loud:

> *"Are you tired? Worn out? Burned out on religion? Come to me. Get away with me and you'll recover your life. I'll show you how to take a real rest. Walk with me and work with me—watch how I do it. Learn the unforced rhythms of grace."*

True joy

Tracy is one of my most inspiring and loving friends. She teaches me so much, especially on rest. In a conversation we had on social media, she said, "Rest makes joy true." My mind began to swirl. She continued, "Rest confirms the fullness of our humanity. In rest our motives are tested." She reminded me that in the creation story, we were brought onto the scene and then immediately invited to rest with the Lord. He worked for six days, and then chose to celebrate by resting with his treasured creation.

True joy doesn't come from how high we've built our tower, but in the intimate bond with our Creator. True joy isn't when our lives and successes are projected out for the world to see, but when we're locked in the gaze of our loving Father. True joy isn't rushed and fleeting, it's constant and unlimited. In rest we experience true joy.

The rest of the story

Your story is not complete without rest. If your joy is rooted in Jesus, then we must follow Jesus into rest. Our rest tells the story that:

- I have all that I need.

- I am loved without striving to earn it.
- My father in heaven is my provider.
- My time is blessed.
- God is sovereign, I can be at peace.
- The world will continue to turn without me.
- I am limited and that's OK.

But it can be challenging! There are many obstacles that keep us from resting. Often, when we do begin to rest, the things we need to bring before the Lord most immediately rise to the surface. We often resist the calm and quiet because it's in the chaos and congestion where we hide and avoid the painful issues (this is why we dug into healing earlier). We may feel shame for resting and taking time away from the needs of those around us, or we may struggle to accept the reality of our limitations. Rest gives us an opportunity to rewrite our story.

You have probably seen or heard the famous Bible verse, "Be still and know that I am God." It's taken from Psalm 46:10. The whole psalm is a description of the work of God on earth. It highlights his protection, defense, power, and great might, not his rest. The rest of the story is that we can "be still" because God is on the job. Knowing who God is and what he does, helps us settle down, inhale in confidence and exhale peace.

How-to

This is a great time to remind you that the invitation to rest flows from God's love for you. It is not something we must do to gain God's favor. There are no strict rules to follow in order for the Father to be pleased. Remember, Jesus was not a fan of the Pharisees who considered themselves to be the Sabbath police. If the idea of an entire 24-hour period is just not possible for you right now, start smaller. Find one morning or night a week to set aside as your sabbath, and then try to find two 24- hour periods a month.

The word "Sabbath" is from the Hebrew word, "Shabbat," which means "To cease." Rest isn't numbing out, binge watching, and endless scrolling. Rest isn't laboring, but it doesn't have to be sedentary. It will look different for everyone so I can't tell you exactly how to rest, but I can give you some parameters.

A good place to start is to evaluate your work. If you work with your hands, rest with your mind. If you work with your mind, rest with your hands. For some, the thought of sitting alone in a quiet room doing nothing for a day is torture, for others, that's bliss. It will be different for everyone. Rest shouldn't feel like captivity. It can be creative and fun. Rest must include joy.

A friend of mine was telling me how she was "supposed" to be having a sabbath but instead she wanted to put together a birdhouse. She asked, "What's a godly thing I should do?" I said, "What do you want to do that will bring you joy?" "Put together this cute birdhouse!" she said. I replied, "Well, then invite the Lord to do it with you and that's the godliest thing you could do right now!" There are certain things attributed to godliness and holiness (worship music, scripture, communion, etc.) but the Lord isn't limited to revealing his love and goodness to those things. The Lord is present. He is near. He is everywhere and can be part of everything we do.

The point of a sabbath rest is to slow down, heighten your awareness of the presence of God, be filled with gratitude and delight, bless your loved ones, and enjoy being loved. Rest in the presence of the Lord is where we are met by love, filled with joy, and strengthened by peace. I love what F.B Meyer says, "Joy is peace dancing. Peace is joy at rest."

You may find great joy in reading, or gardening, doing a puzzle with your family, or sharing a meal with your friends (my personal favorite!). Rest may look like taking a walk and noticing things you've never seen before, praying for your neighborhood, and being aware of the beauty of creation. You may find joy in sleeping too, that's great! I love Psalm 149:5, which says, "Let the faithful rejoice that he honors them. Let them sing for joy as they lie on their beds. "Yes, please! I am happy to sing for joy as I lie in bed.

JOYFUL DISCOVERY

FOMO. The fear of missing out. It's a thing! I remember having a conversation with the Lord lamenting about how I felt I was missing out on the good stuff that was happening while I was at home, "resting." I was being a "good girl" and yet feeling like I was missing the good stuff. God was so gracious and kind to me. He lovingly said, "You're not missing out on what they're doing! They're missing out on what *we're* doing!" He was right. I had the full attention of my loving Father and he had beauty, revelation, and an abundance of joy to give me. My FOMO became JOMO, the joy of missing out.

Playtime

When was the last time you played? I don't mean on your phone or PlayStation, I mean sheer, unproductive, unplugged fun. Play is an art most people lose with time, but it's proven to be extremely beneficial to our well-being. (I know, I just said it was supposed to be unproductive, so let's agree to call it both). Scientific studies have shown that nothing fires up the brain like play. It stimulates all kinds of positive activity throughout our system and has amazing outcomes. Dr. Stuart Brown has created the National Institute for Play. His TED talks, books, studies, and articles are fascinating. He has studied animals, children, adults, and murderers. His conclusion is "the opposite of play isn't work, it's depression."[1]

Because most of us have lost the art of play, it begs the question, how do we define play? If the purpose is more important than doing it, it's probably not play. Play jumps, skips, runs, tackles and tickles, tinkers, and colors. Play tells stories, daydreams, and celebrates. When done with others, play creates bonds, crosses barriers, and cultivates community. When done alone, play expands our imagination and supports the release of our self-conscious inhibitions.

The art of play is serious business because it helps to keep us on the right path. When we deprive ourselves of natural, healthy play and fun, we look to the more sinister and destructive options. We long to have an "escape." We numb our minds and suppress our feelings by bingeing endless hours of meaningless shows. We scroll to observe and escape, judging and coveting other people's lives. These things aren't actually helping in any way. It only delays the inevitable. We will eventually "deal" with our pent-up frustrations, pain, shame and unhappiness, but most often in an even more destructive way.

Secrets live and thrive in the dark. As we get older, we often exchange good clean fun with a dark and destructive imposter. But the effect is not the same in our bodies and brains. Dr. Brown says, "Play helps us belong in the community, develop the ability to sup-

---

1   Quote Source: https://neuroscience.stanford.edu/news/opposite-play-not-work-it-depression

press unwanted urges, and regulate our emotions." Play is vital to our health and a great tool to lead ourselves and others well.

Rest in joy

Jesus rested in joy. The joy of his identity. He knew who he was, a son not a slave. He rested in the joy of the love of his father. A father who was present, powerful, and delighted by his son. He rested in the joy of abundance, knowing no lack because he had access to all of the riches of heaven. And Jesus rested with confidence. He was not fooled by the deceiver but at peace and confident in the truth.

I bless you to rest in joy. Use this Joy Bringer's Core Value to lead yourself and others well. You are worthy of rest because you are a child of the Most High King. He is pleased with you and wants you to be filled with his joy so that you can bring it with you wherever you go.

JOY BRINGER CHALLENGE

Part A: I challenge you to take a step toward rest. No matter where you are, just take one step forward. If you have no intentional rest in your week and seemingly no room for some, start by scheduling a half a day next week. If you have a day off, label it as a sabbath day and protect it. Be proactive about adding consistent rest to your schedule.

Part B: "It's all up to me!" The enemy would have you believe that you must continue to pile on more and more just to make it through the day. The more you pick up, the more weighted down you become. I challenge you to let some things go. Consider taking these steps:

- Identify a list of things that you feel totally and completely responsible for.
- Now, let's ask the Lord what He would have you hold onto and where there are invitations for you to let them go or pass them onto someone else.
- And, finally, ask the Lord what he is going to give you in order to handle the things you are assigned to manage. Ask how he will equip you to do it with joy.

Remember: The Lord is looking at you, gazing at you with love and delight. I challenge you to spend some time just looking back at him. Rest in his gaze of love.

_____

_____

_____

_____

_____

_____

_____

_____

_____

Afterword:

A Joy Bringer's Blessing

Joy verse

"May the God of hope fill you with all joy and peace as you
trust in him, so that you may overflow with hope by the power
of the Holy Spirit."–Romans 15:13 NIV

I am one of the gazillion people who have left California and
relocated to the south. As a new Tennessee resident, I am getting
acquainted with the nuance of the phrase, "Bless your heart."
It's a multifunctional term. It can be used when you are feeling
compassion and love toward someone, or when you want to
comment on one's stupidity but do it with a smile. Blessing
someone isn't just reserved for the southerner, or after a sneeze.
Scripture says the power of a blessing lasts for generations. Blessing
is simply adding value to someone's life.

It is my prayer that this challenge adds immense value to your
life. Thank you for allowing me to lead you through this process. I
trust that you have been met by love and grown in your awareness
of the presence and power of the Lord in your life. I pray that you
are not the same. I pray that you have new tools, experiences, and

perspectives to help you live powered by the good news. And I bless you, dear reader.

I bless you to receive life-changing and life-giving love from your heavenly Father and be marked by gratitude. I bless you to continue to heal. To say yes to the deeper revelations of wholeness and goodness and forgive because the Lord has forgiven you. I bless you to experience the fresh wind and fire of the Holy Spirit and be flexible to follow his lead. I bless you to be buoyant with joy, fixing your eyes on the Good Shepherd who will lead you with delight to places of victory, rest, and joy. And "May the God of hope fill you with all joy and peace as you trust in him, so that you may overflow with hope by the power of the Holy Spirit" (Romans 15:13 NIV).

I would love to hear about your journey! Please connect with me and share your experience with me. You can find me at my website seasonbowers.com or on social media.

Now go, Joy Bringer, and live the power of the good news!

About the author

After more than 20 years as a professional actor on the stage telling good stories well, Season retired from the theatre to tell the best story well. Whether on the radio, speaking on large or small platforms, in writing, or over a long lunch, Season loves any opportunity to connect with people and talk about Jesus. Transparent through the difficulties of life she makes a daily and even moment-to-moment choice to lock eyes  with Jesus as her source of hope and constant joy. She can be heard on radio stations across the country through her daily feature, Joy Bringer. She has a MDiv from Bethel Seminary San Diego and is ordained through the Free Methodist denomination. Thanks to Christianmingle.com she met her husband Kris and they married ten weeks later giving Season the greatest gift of becoming an insta-mom to Aubrey, Alana and Aireana. Season and her husband travel as much as possible but call Knoxville, Tennessee home. While full of joy and Jesus, Season is almost always full of tea with maybe too much creamer which she only drinks through a straw.

A free ebook edition
is available with the
purchase of this book.

To claim your free ebook edition:

1. Visit MorganJamesBOGO.com
2. Sign your name CLEARLY in the space
3. Complete the form and submit a photo of
   the entire copyright page
4. You or your friend can download the ebook
   to your preferred device

Morgan James
BOGO™

A **FREE** ebook edition is available for you
or a friend with the purchase of this print book.

CLEARLY SIGN YOUR NAME ABOVE

Instructions to claim your free ebook edition:
1. Visit MorganJamesBOGO.com
2. Sign your name CLEARLY in the space above
3. Complete the form and submit a photo
   of this entire page
4. You or your friend can download the ebook
   to your preferred device

Print & Digital Together Forever.

Snap a photo

Free ebook

Read anywhere

CPSIA information can be obtained
at www.ICGtesting.com
Printed in the USA
JSHW080428220723
45207JS00001B/1